A Walk with Lady Wisdom

A Walk with Lady Wisdom

Eric J. Epstein

A Walk with Lady Wisdom
Copyright © 2020 by Eric J. Epstein

Illustrations by Tara Chávez

ISBN-13: 978-1-7350318-0-4

Printed in the United States of America

For my wife, Elise Epstein

What we have been given—
through bounties of beauty and grace,
through nearly unspeakable suffering,
through journeys no one could have anticipated,
we are united and held gently and firmly.

TABLE OF CONTENTS

FOREWORD

I first met Eric in 2006, when he was working as a counselor at my rural Southern Oregon high school. I was a confused, artistic adolescent searching for my voice. I spent the summer competing in a national speech tournament, then a month in Boston at a precollege program for the arts. Home after that felt empty and lonely. The last of my four older siblings had left the once lively house, and I had perhaps already outlived my usefulness. I sought out Eric when a family friend passed away, jolting me out of the dull penetrating depression that had consumed me since returning home. He authentically listened to me and gave me a respect not often extended to youth. He helped me through that moment and imbued the seeds of self-belief that would evolve into the courage to pursue my dreams in the visual arts.

When Eric asked me to illustrate a book he wrote, I was in a very different but resonant place. Building my life as an illustrator in France, fresh out of an abusive marriage, I was starting to feel solid again after my life fell to pieces. Throughout everything, trauma would frequently sneak up and snatch away my sense of self. When isolation in a foreign country brought up old questions of my worth and purpose, I had often gone back to the early message Eric left me: that I needn't search for a voice, I just need to believe in the voice I have. The idea of helping Eric share insights like this with a wider audience thrilled me. I have never said yes to a project faster.

Illustrating the book was a powerful and personal process. I deeply related to the stories of these strong women, each of whom the book approaches as unique individuals with particular personal histories. My heart ached for many of them, my mind circled around the epiphanies they reached with Eric, their understandings highlighted by the poetic meaningful way he found to weave the stories together. The writing is similar to the strange way life lays different situations on us, sometimes so surreal that all you can do is laugh until you find meaning in the mystery. Moments of unveiled understanding illuminated some overlooked dark corners of my own workings. The shame I still struggle to understand, the guilt I feel for allowing myself to be in a dangerous home. What does it take to be a woman who understands she can be hurt, be lost, but find she is still powerful, still strong?

It is not always easy for us to see ourselves clearly. Sometimes you are lucky enough to meet someone with the genuine capacity to reflect back the positive parts of yourself that you have pushed away. Someone who not only reflects your strengths back to you, but also actively helps you see all the good, the hurting, and the hidden. Eric is one such individual, and his impact is not only to help people see their potential, but how we can then do the same for others. We all switch roles, counselor to client, the empathetic ear to the lost voice yearning for some recognition. This book is a gift of both perspectives, and I have been honored to participate in its creation, and to be on this journey with all of us seeking Lady Wisdom.

—Tara Chávez

I

WISDOM & RECIPROCAL DIGNITY

It should be no surprise that many ancient civilizations viewed
wisdom as a woman.
She is linked to the foundation of life, beauty, and existence.
She brings nurture, meaning, understanding, and humility – the basis
of seeing.

She must be pursued and cannot be possessed.
To move with her requires letting go of oneself and being caught up in
that which is vast, tender, intimate, and beyond.

2015 Colorado, USA

After completing a hard move back to Colorado, I did not have a job. We had uprooted our change-resistant family in the course of seven rough weeks and left our home of fifteen years in the woods of Oregon. We were disrupted financially, adrift relationally, and unmoored nearly to the core. Reacquainting with people and places that had changed after we had left nearly two decades prior, we found ourselves mired in the effort required to begin again. Our children were rejected from multiple schools, and as we explored places to root ourselves, I remained unsure what I would do for work.

We had taken this uncharacteristic step because of a single *no*. We had been looking for a more just way of life, and so for twenty years we considered joining an intentional community. After hosting many of their members and living with them for short visits, they compassionately told us *no*—we were not meant to join them. It should have felt like rejection, but surprisingly it didn't. A sudden clarity came to me, instead—we were to move to Colorado. I don't tend to receive clear direction fully developed like this, and I do not make fast decisions that could potentially hurt people. And yet it happened anyway, and we knew we had to move to Colorado right away. It was where my wife and I had grown up, where family and friends still lived, and where better school options existed for our children, but the clarity did not come from these things.

And so there we were, living off the income from my wife's part-time, near-minimum-wage job in an area where the cost of living was high. It was the first time she had been able to work since our now teenage children were born and we were grateful, but fiscally very lean. We tried to be ready—but for what?

Part of why I didn't have a job was that I was looking for something I wasn't sure existed. I had been connected to multiple organizations in Oregon which had healing and educational competency which was suddenly lost when individuals departed or systems changed. I struggled to understand why this happened, but I recognized the symptoms. I had previously worked with some international development organizations with wonderful missions and relationships around the world, and I had watched many of them cause unintended harm and fail to cultivate a healthy internal culture. It seemed to me that the common element in these organizations' fragility and blindness had to do with a lack of wisdom.

Now in Colorado, I spent my time looking for that wisdom. I met with anyone I could find who would talk with me about work related to wisdom, but I quietly doubted anything would come of it. Wisdom is hard to understand. Attempting to discover how it could be cultivated, held, honored, or passed on revealed more of what was not being done than what was. But I held onto a fragile belief that scattered experiences from my previous work in business, education, and health could be somehow melded into a form I once experienced in India.

1996 MUMBAI, INDIA

I was in Mumbai with the mission to evaluate the young businesses of some men who were trying to lift their village out of poverty. Lenders in America had supported these businesses with microloans, the idea being that recipients would support each other to make sure their loans were repaid, making those funds available again for new projects. This was one of my first tastes of a mutually-beneficial, dignity-reinforcing model and it influenced much of what I tried to do for work since then.

After thirty hours of travel, I was welcomed into the home of a lovely Indian couple who had done many development projects in India and who guided, translated, and lead this effort. They showed me how giving and receiving dignity could accomplish the seemingly impossible. Initially, I was overwhelmed by the hospitality, not only of my hosts, but of the village too. My hosts let me use their bed when rats and cobras inside the walls of my guest house kept me awake. The villagers treated me like a dignitary, placing a turban on my head, blessing me with oils and symbolic objects, and even bowing and kissing my feet. I was given a coconut by a family that might have had only that one for the entire year. I tried to protest that this was all too much and not needed, but everyone insisted that it was their honor to treat me this way, that to reject it would be to reject them. They called me Sahib, "great one," and I slowly learned that they held many beliefs about white people that were a strange legacy of British occupation. Some thought we could not be in the sun while others thought we could not run or lift heavy objects, and so I tried to intentionally do these things to challenge their overly-elevated view of me. I once tried calling some of the men Sahib, and they did not like it. So I called them "brother" and asked them to do the same with me, which was slowly accepted.

During one meeting, I listed some things that Americans did not do as well as they did: their marriages stayed together when ours fell apart more frequently, they had festivals that brought people together more than we did, and they could call upon the help of their neighbors with much greater ease and availability. After explaining these things in a translated discussion, a muscled water buffalo rancher named Vishnu stood up and said, "When I get enough money, I will travel to America and help you with your marriages, festivals, and neighborhoods because you have helped us with our businesses." The fierceness and strength in his expressions moved me, and when I shared these stories with the American lenders, they wanted to further support this step toward mutuality.

When I returned to the United States, I wondered why this experience had affected me so much. I doubted that Vishnu would ever be able to really address the issues we had discussed, but something had shifted in him that was new and vital. It brought to mind a story we had been told about another organization also trying to economically lift an Indian coastal village whose main commodity was shrimp. They had given new technology to some of the shrimping boat owners which allowed them to catch far more shrimp than ever before. The result at first seemed to be a success. This test group made quite a bit more money; they bought more supplies from the local economy, and the village benefitted. So this organization gave the technology to more boat owners, but within two years the shrimpers who were more successful than the others crushed the remaining competition, depleted the shrimp supply, dominated the area, and then moved out of the village to live in nicer places, taking their "economic benefit" with them. They had absorbed competitive, consumer values and practices which had not been intentionally taught by their "helping" organization. I wondered whether things might have turned out differently if this group of men had an experience like Vishnu's.

2015 Colorado, USA

I felt a little reckless and irresponsible spending so much time meeting with people in coffee shops, parks, and offices just to talk about these ideas when our income was so small. I sensed that the concept of mutuality, or what later became reciprocal dignity, was somehow connected to wisdom, and I was almost haunted by the desire to understand and embrace it.

During my years in Oregon, I had danced around the edges and blurred the boundaries of standard health and learning practices in the arenas of business, education, and mental health. The results had coalesced into multiple forms, all experimenting with ways to help people grow in health and wisdom. Like most start-ups, there were more failures and opportunities for learning than there were first-time successes. One of the companies grew to employ a wonderful team of people for five years, but it rapidly diminished within one year when the entire team was hit by life circumstances that caused them each to quit one by one. Another was a school-based initiative that grew to serve fifteen schools. Not long after receiving national funding potential, it was misunderstood by the organization it was operating under and slowly diminished into oblivion.

These legacies had created a hunger in me to find a better way. Now that I was in Colorado and on my own again, I could start from scratch. Again. It was humbling to be at a stage of life when many of my peers were well-established, but I held onto a little hope that using what I had learned might produce something more enduring than my past work had.

The scattered meetings began to coalesce into two forms of work:

- Consulting with individuals, couples, and families in a form that resembled counseling.

- Consulting with organizations to utilize their own intentionally gathered wisdom to navigate transitions.

In the first type of work, people came to me with a wide variety of problems and with the expectation that I would help solve them. They often brought their diagnoses and previous failed attempts, trying to determine whether I was worth investing time and money in from the minute they walked in the door. Since I was operating as a consultant, I had maximum freedom to try anything that seemed helpful.

To my joy and surprising contentment, something new constantly happened in this practice that I can only describe as sacred. My clients and I kept experiencing strong, vital understanding and inner change formed by the junction of our best qualities. It reminded me of Vishnu in India.

The science lover in me wanted to understand what was happening in our sessions so I could consistently re-create the conditions for lasting change. Some of my clients wanted to understand what was happening too, to have a name for it, or at least a way to talk about it. But I didn't fully understand how it was occurring, and I had a hard time even describing it. In trying to avoid being a professional counselor, I had fallen into something else. I needed some perspective, so I asked for some help.

2016 COLORADO, A FRIEND'S BACKYARD

One summer day, I was hanging out in a tree house with two male friends who had far more formal psychological training than I did, talking and enjoying each other's company. As the conversation moved from lighter to deeper, the question began to burn inside me. Feeling awkward, I blurted out, "Could you guys help me figure out what kind of counseling I am doing?"

They asked me to describe what it was like when I met with people. As I talked, they'd say, "That sounds like positive psychology"; "Really, that's more like solution-based therapy"; "Well, that part is very cognitive behavioral, even though the way you did it was unusual." As they worked sincerely to give me an answer, I felt discouraged. These were smart guys and they knew me well. Their answers were good but somehow not what I needed. I heard in their suggestions the inherent power difference and lack of reciprocity built into psychological practice, which did not fit what I was doing.

An idea hit me later that seemed so obvious I felt foolish: I could interview the people who had been through the process with me and had experienced the mutual transformation first hand—my "clients."

This idea became a fruitful reality. Not only did the interviews begin to open my eyes, they also brought new healing and growth to the participants. When we explored how they had overcome their hardships we discovered, from the vantage point of the future, new significance and meaning that we had not seen at the time. Often there were parts of their lives they had not told me about during our sessions that they now revealed. Sometimes there were things that still held them back, and we were better able to grapple with them now that time had passed. I even began to see some of my past work with individual recovery in a new light that further clarified this practice of reciprocal dignity. As we talked, our interviews became more like dialogues, and I was surprised that the people who could best articulate this "other way of doing counseling" were nearly all women. It was happening as frequently with men, but they seemed to have a harder time explaining it. It reminded me of the initial experiences in India where I was given so much respect, it became a barrier to the growth of all involved.

These deeply-seeing women I talked to had all experienced tremendous suffering and left me with two questions: How had these women found their healing? Why had being with them changed me?

A theme emerged early on as the women tried to explain what had happened between and within us: "We made each other better"; "You were the right person at the right time to fit with me"; "We were at the table together." This *union in the process* was what I was reaching for but couldn't easily locate within the traditional counseling models which places the focus on the professional's skills. The women carefully articulated that the connection between us was not sloppy, needy, or unhealthy; rather, the connections were deeply respectful, and this made them empowering.

The women's answers reminded me of what I had learned in my amateur study of philosophy and spiritual traditions—that wisdom often comes through relationships and dialogue, the latter of which included both inner and outer conversations. I view study and self-reflection as inner conversations and living relationships as outer conversations. When given some important conditions these conversations can produce meaningful realizations and change.

The respect required for this kind of dialogue and mutuality comes close to reverence, though some aspects of the people involved may not seem worthy of respect. Often elements such as silence, laughter, understanding, shared purpose, and joyful activity have new meaning when they are oriented toward developing this kind of connection.

Relationships and discoveries of this kind were limited when I worked in organizations that focused on the professionals having answers for the sufferers. My experiences have taught me that a community cannot grow on the back of an expert—that a person thinking of themselves as an expert often defeats the long-term growth process. There cannot be a union of perspectives or co-creation when one side of the relationship is structurally undervalued.

WHAT TO EXPECT NEXT

Let's exit my story for a little while so you can engage with this book a bit more proactively. As you have probably figured out by now, this book is not exactly a psychological or self-help book, though there are elements of both within. I have taken certain liberties with how I tell the following stories, both to protect the real people involved and to guide you through a process of discovery. I'm trying to emulate reciprocal dignity in text, giving you some tools that may feel unfamiliar or awkward at first, but that might help you do your own work better than if you viewed me as the "expert" with all the answers. Maybe these tools will work for you; maybe they won't. Both outcomes are fine—finding what does and does not fit you is important to this process. Hopefully you'll walk away with a little more wisdom that *you've* discovered.

This book includes interviews with six women, which in no small measure is the story of how their lives blended with mine. You could view these stories as psychological case studies, but don't do that. There are deeper elements occurring here that need to be found.

For each story, I will help identify the trap that each woman was caught in; two liberating, proverb-like "wisdom nuggets" that I have discovered in each story (one for counsel-providers and one for anyone who wants to grow); and a dialogue that shows how the nuggets work. Do your own digging to find additional treasures in these stories and you may find how reciprocal dignity can set the stage for wisdom.

I've also written short poems to introduce each story; they are dense and symbolic of the inner lessons I learned, but they are not for everyone. Pass them by if they don't fit you.

I am not advocating for all counsel-oriented professionals to operate as I do. In fact, that would likely be quite bad. The road I walk is hard and could be harmful if the walker does not fit the road.

One could say that the struggles these women faced while meeting with me should be kept private and that my writing about them is a violation. I take this issue seriously—each of these women were encouraged to pull the plug on sharing their story at any time, and some considered doing so. Some felt like they should have their lives more together so they could offer a happy ending to inspire others. One had to go to bed and recover after reading her story in print for the first time.

All were encouraged to hide their identity to protect themselves, but one said, "You're damn well going to use my real name and tell the world this story! I paid for it with a lot of pain and everyone will know that it is mine." She eventually agreed to hide her identity to protect others connected to her. As we finalized the manuscript, many of the women felt fear about some of the rougher details of their lives being out in the world. The need for additional edits and protections became clear. Some of the women initially felt burdensome in their requests to take the time to make sure their voices were clear, the precautions solid, and the risks understood. As this time and care was taken, even more realizations and healing occurred in all of us.

These women remain my friends. Some would consider this a violation of professional ethics; I do not, as long as specific criteria are met (see Appendix E). There are real risks when roles are not predetermined, and in the majority of situations the systems set up to prevent misuse of power are helpful to avoid the confusion of dual relationships, giving or receiving gifts, or transference (of personal matters to a client inappropriately). However, the uncommon potential for fruitful friendship between myself and the women with whom I work is one of the primary reasons I have chosen to operate outside the medical model. One question this book wrestles with is, *Are there situations where wise friendship is necessary for healing?*

In the midst of this writing, I paused and wondered, "Why should a man write about women?" One friend helped me with the words: "It's good to begin with women because they are usually at the start of anything living and good." Another said, "A man writing about women can help both women and men." Sometimes we are too close to something to see it—it's too familiar. Because I am not a woman, perhaps I can appreciate these women in ways they can't as easily appreciate themselves.

It is a beautiful mystery that in helping women be a more whole expression of their feminine selves, they have helped me be a better man. They were not only a gift during my struggle to express what I was doing; they helped me see what other women in my life—my mother, wife, and daughter—were giving to me and what I was giving to them. In the end, it also changed how I view men and even my own masculinity.

I also paused to better understand how this long effort would affect my wife by teasingly asking, "So how come you're supportive of me spending all this time with other women?" Of course she had to tease me back: "Because I am the best wife ever," and "It's good to share what you have." But in the end, when she spoke of "our life ethic" to do and honor this kind of relating, I could rest in her trust that this was worth doing.

As I've suggested before, wisdom is the central theme of this book— and yet how many people do you know who you would consider wise? Although I have lamented the loss and lack of wisdom in my culture, I would prefer to find ways to cultivate it and pass it on. I have experienced few organizations that make honoring and passing on their existing and emerging wisdom a central practice. Let's change that.

II

EMOTIONS DON'T EXIST

A Dream of Wise Counsel
I reach into the hidden, the dark, the afraid – rage greets me – pain
screams,
I know them and do not waver.
Voices echo in pale, sweaty circles with no tone – they blend – they
hide in thought,
I reveal them and their cowardice.
They run to softer places and begin their death spirals once again.

MY HOME

Psyche Journal *wants me to do an interview regarding a practice that our team of counselors and consultants have been using called reciprocal dignity. It came about because I described this practice to my editor, Cecillia, over coffee while discussing this book. The concept made her think of a friend, Janelle, who works for* Psyche *and is interested in methods for helping suffering people that don't create dependency or power separation. Cecillia called her, told her about it, and she wanted to know where the concept of reciprocal dignity came from. I sent Janelle the above introduction, hoping she'd want more.*

She did!

Exciting! My book isn't even finished, and they're already interested in some of the core ideas! Cecillia said to go ahead and give them the next six stories and some accompanying elements which flesh out the relationship between wisdom and reciprocal dignity, so I sent what I had even though I hadn't written the connections between the stories yet. The following is the first story in the six I sent; it's first because it inspired me to ask why I was I receiving so much (when I was the one who was supposed to be the "professional giver.")

I am working in rural high schools and conducting an experiment involving teen girls and self-hate. So many think poorly of themselves, and it surprises me because I see them so differently. I select ten random girls and invite them to tell me about their strengths. We list them, draw them, talk about them, or whatever it takes to find them. I start by putting a blank piece of paper in front of each girl and ask her to write down her best qualities. All ten respond as if this is very hard; most of them can't write more than three items, and many get stuck at one. They write qualities and then cross them out because "they aren't strengths all the time" and "sometimes they are weaknesses." I appreciate the maturity and humility required to accept such perspectives, but as time goes on I realize every girl in the group is significantly held back from pursuing the life they would like to live because of how they see themselves.

I can't believe it. What kind of crazy mind trick has made these beautiful, intelligent, strong girls think they don't have good qualities? I talk to colleagues about it and hear many cultural answers that don't seem to explain fully what the girls face. I commit to spending more time with them to find the missing pieces.

General "self-esteem" education and people saying nice things to these girls does almost nothing. I call them "compliment ninjas" because they are so good at chopping positive statements to pieces before they can receive them. Even those that know their good qualities, put them aside as irrelevant under certain conditions. I sense that finding the way out of this trap will require a depth of understanding and relationship with these young women that is hard to achieve at a school. I sense I could change some conditions in order to increase the chances of this happening. I have a chance to follow my intuition when a sophomore honors student slowly extends the trust needed for me to see the bindweeds choking her heart and mind.

★

I am handed a hastily written note telling me to pull a student named Kim out of class for an unspecified issue. When I arrive outside her classroom, I send someone else in with the note so that it won't be obvious she is heading to counseling. Kim comes out and her eye movements show me how exceptionally observant she is, how quickly her mind moves. She is short with dark hair; vibrant, dark eyes take me in before quickly looking down.

"This is a mistake," she says. "I don't really need anything. I just wanted to try out the Student Services system, but you probably have other more important things to do."

"Well, I'm here," I say. "And I don't have anything pressing. It's fine with me if we meet."

"No, I should really get back to class. Sorry."

I feel strongly that if I do not talk with Kim now, I will not talk with her ever again.

"Since I came here and you're already out of class, why don't we just talk a little, and then I won't bug you anymore if you don't want me to? We don't even have to go to my office. We can just walk a few times around the track."

She scrutinizes me and then gives in. Much later, Kim tells me that without this option, it would have all ended there.

"Okay. But I won't take much of your time."

We head to the track in awkward silence. I feel her scrutinizing me again, and she seems to be planning how to get through this conversation as quickly as possible.

After extensive prodding, Kim reveals that she likes math and performing musically—playing the piano and singing. She's very close to her younger sister and is protective of her. Grades are good, parents are good—everything else is basically good.

"So, you're pretty happy with life, then…?" I say slowly, thinking that I'm about to lose her and haven't found what I need to find.

"Happiness is kind of dumb, don't you think?"

"What do you mean?"

"Well, emotions are basically made up in our minds, and if we want to get things done, we should just stop working so hard to be happy or stop being sad or whatever. Like when I do math: I could get all caught up in how slow the pace of the class is, or how I wish I was somewhere else, or I could do harder problems that would challenge me. But that's all just a distraction. I just need to do the math. If we live knowing that emotions are illusions, it's a lot better."

"Wow. So, are you saying the things that emotions are connected to aren't real either? Like love or justice or beauty?"

"Love is basically just the biological drive to breed or wanting to be with someone because they let you do what you want to do. It's all in your head or in your hormones. If you see it for what it is, it's much less annoying."

"So emotions were annoying and you got rid of them?"

"Pretty much. They still come up now and then, but I know how to get around them."

"If I said I was impressed by how much you've thought about this, then I would just be captured by dumb feelings?"

A half-grin pops up on Kim's face, and then she shakes her head.

"You can think things like that. Just don't make them into a big deal. Drama is everywhere, and it's pretty stupid to let yourself get caught up in it. I doubt these thoughts are all that uncommon. If anyone stops and looks at life, they could see how much trouble emotions cause."

Something seems to bother her when she hears that statement out loud, but she tries to hide it.

I ask, "What kind of trouble have you seen?"

"Don't get all psychoanalytical on me. I knew I shouldn't have said that last bit. I just meant that lots of people let their emotions lead them around, and then they act stupid."

"Okay. So, you're telling me that your life is better now that you don't let emotions get in the way?"

"Yep."

"And everything is good?"

"Yes."

I try to think of some other topic to pursue casually, but something feels wrong—something bad is happening. Just then, she smiled a nice little triumphant smile.

"Can I go back to class now? I really should get some work done. It was nice to meet you."

"Sure. Nice to meet you too. Why don't we plan to talk again next week? I think your no-emotion philosophy is interesting!"

"No. I think I wasted enough of your time. Can you sign my pass, please? Thanks. See you around."

And she walked away.

It felt like she wanted to skip victoriously but held herself to a brisk walk. Why did I feel so bad when she seemed to be happy? What just happened?

The brief exchange stuck in my head, heart, and gut with a roiling turbulence that did not diminish. I had to find a way to keep our conversation going. I also felt that the harder I tried to make it happen, the more she would drift away.

I checked myself. Why did I have such a strong desire to talk with her? I had the strange feeling that she was about to die, and she was smiling at death.

It felt like I needed to somehow wake her up, but she wanted to sleep. I decided to give her (and myself) some time and then try to talk with her next week.

The following week, I tried to pick a class that she could afford to miss and sent out a pass for her to come see me. And then I waited. I doubted she would come. I almost sent out a pass for another student, thinking I might look like I was slacking if I sat in my office too long without anyone to meet with. And then Kim walked into my office with her funny half-smile, shaking her head at how foolish I was.

"What do you want to talk about now? I think we covered pretty much everything."

She was trying to make me second-guess myself. She wanted me to leave her alone, because I had no business getting involved. But her face said, *You're such a silly guy. Let's have a laugh at your silly thoughts.*

"Hi, Kim! Come on in. I'm looking forward to my next lesson on the Emotions Are Illusions philosophy! Is now a good time?"

She shrugged and sat down. For an instant, I thought I saw a flash of gladness on her face. It was gone so fast, I wondered if I had really seen it.

"I thought that we could start by coming up with some situations to test your philosophy and see how well it stands. I have a few things to throw at you, and maybe you could throw some situations at me. I'll try to defend those poor emotions you're trying to get rid of, and you can show me where I'm falling into illusions? Sound good?"

"Sure..." She raised a skeptical eyebrow. My gut told me she was actually interested and wanted to defeat me at this game.

"Okay. So, have you ever been interested in someone where your hormones weren't the driving force? Like you really felt a connection to them in a way that might be called love?"

"Well, I'm very loyal to my family. I'll protect them no matter what. But that isn't love, that's just logical, because they're a big part of my life and it makes sense to keep that going. I've been attracted to guys, but it's usually stupid. They're fun to flirt and hang out with, but I won't ever marry or have kids."

"Why not?"

"I want to use my math skills to accomplish important things and not be held back by a husband or kids. I don't really like kids that much anyway. They're so emotion driven, it's kind of gross."

This struck me as not the full story. I needed to stop being the question-asker, because I knew she had a low tolerance for "counseling." It was her turn.

"Do you want to bounce anything off me?"

After a long pause, she finally said, "If I tell you something hypothetically, you don't have to do anything about it, right?"

"If I have reason to believe that abuse or neglect are happening, I have to report it. I will also have to do something if a person tells me they're going to hurt themselves or someone else."

"But if it's hypothetical, we can just talk about it, and you'd have nothing to report, right?"

This young lady knew the limits and was walking right up to them. "That's true. If we start to cross the line where I suspect something real is happening, I'll tell you, okay?"

She stared at me for just a moment, but even this was clearly calculated. She wanted me to know she would be watching me, but not that she had anything to hide.

"Okay," she said. "Let's say there is a teenage boy, and he's always getting on his parent's nerves, but he basically doesn't get in any trouble at school. If he says he's worried about his brother to a counselor, could a counselor talk about the situation rationally, or would they have to rush off and meet with the brother?"

My mind jumped to her sister. "I think a counselor could just talk about it if there wasn't any pressing danger. How does this relate to your philosophy?"

"Because counselors are *obsessed* with feelings! And I don't want to talk with you if you're like that."

Wow. What a challenge. In many ways she was right. I had a running joke with a counselor friend in which we would look at each other with starry eyes and say, "How does that make you feel?" Kim had just turned the game on me. I had to talk with her in hypotheticals without focusing on emotions, while trying to understand—without acknowledging—the massive burden she seemed to be carrying. I was excited to play.

"Wow. Let's go back to your scenario. What was the brother worried about?"

I tried to be practical in my tone because she might think "worry" was an emotion, and then I would be kicked out of the game.

"The older brother is worried about the younger one leaving for college, because the younger one is used to the older brother protecting him. The younger brother is very innocent and doesn't get how dangerous the world is. That's part of what's wonderful about him, but also what could really be a problem."

"What kind of danger is most likely?"

"Oh, any kind. Girls are after him who might make him love them even though they're bad for him. Guys might want to beat him up because he isn't as big as everyone else. His parents might surprise him, because up to this point he's been the golden child and could do no wrong. But his parents will probably be harder on him or just disappoint him once the older brother is gone, since the older brother does a lot behind the scenes that isn't recognized by his younger sibling."

"Does the older brother tell any of these things to the younger one?"

"Oh yeah. He just laughs it off and thinks the older brother is overreacting."

"It sounds to me like it would be important to stay connected and spend time together so the older brother could slowly show the younger one what he does to keep things going smoothly instead of just talking about it. If they have a good relationship, they could keep talking during the year and be together during breaks."

"Yeah, but the younger brother sees life all rosy. He might not say when things are bad."

"That's tricky. It sounds like honesty might be part of the problem."

For some reason this struck a chord, and our "hypothetical" discussion suddenly seemed a lot more real. Kim looked at me quizzically.

"Sometimes honesty is overrated."

"How so?"

"I have to go."

"Okay. Shall I send you a pass next week?"

"Maybe. I'll see how things are going. Can you sign this?"

And she left.

I felt strongly that the story was about her sister and her. I felt like she knew that I knew. She wanted to see how I would handle it. Why the trouble about honesty?

Clearly there was something that she didn't want to talk about. Why? Protection of the family? This was starting to look like something bad.

Over the next few months, we continued to meet, and Kim would intrigue and infuriate me with the slow pace of her hypothetical disclosures. She expanded on her "emotions don't exist" theory, explaining that humanity would be better off if people weren't weakened by their "pathetic inability to control their emotions" and simply acted constructively. She had felt it necessary to convince herself that if people wanted to be happy, all they would essentially have to do is portray themselves as happy. They should control their emotions rather than let their emotions control them, just as she was convinced she was doing with her masks. "People are only sad because they are weak-willed. If they really wanted to be happy, they would just be happy and that would be the end of it."

I sensed her consequent cheery exterior was both a courageous façade and a shield. She was protecting herself and others. I would often step bit by bit toward clarity and then she would jump back and claim it was all false. Sometimes I would hint at what I knew, and she would turn into the sphinx or the *Mona Lisa*, giving me nothing more. She was so smart! She was so good at playing this game I would have thought she'd met with a hundred counselors if she hadn't told me otherwise.

Summer soon came, and it seemed as if the surface had barely
been scratched. I worried about her, but felt that it would be too
overwhelming for me to reach out to her during break.

Kim started her junior year with a disposition just as cheery as the
previous year. She approached me within the first couple weeks saying that she had enjoyed our talks from the previous year and would
like to continue them. And so our meetings continued. It was hard
for me to feel her walls back up to full strength, and for our first few
discussions it was the old "keep away from me" dance, but eventually
Kim warmed up again.

A couple months into the school year, there was a day that was
different. I saw Kim walking in the hallway, and she pretended like
she didn't see me. Just as she passed, I noticed a slight yellowness in
the skin next to one of her eyes. For a moment, I imagined it was
an unusual eye shadow, but it didn't fit the whole picture. I turned
around and watched her walk away with a very well-disguised limp. I
wrote a pass requesting that she come see me as soon as possible. After two class periods, she reluctantly came in.

"Hi."

She tried to be positive and normal at the same time. She saw I
didn't buy it.

"What's the deal with your eye?" I asked.

"I was dumb and bashed it with my hair straightener. Is it noticeable? It looks so ugly, I tried to cover it with makeup."

"It looks like a pretty solid black eye if I look closely."

"Yeah."

"How about your leg? It looks like you have a limp."

"Oh, I'm a clod. I tripped down some steps and twisted my ankle. It's no big deal, really."

It felt like she was saying, "Please don't make these things a big deal." I knew that I had seen enough to make a report to Child Protective Services, but I also knew that the trust I'd earned with Kim was fragile and that she would very likely deny anything other than her story. If I had followed the letter of the law, I would have called, and Kim likely would have never talked to me again. I decided to get more information.

"I hope you feel better."

"I don't feel much of anything . . . remember?"

"And that's working right now?"

"Well enough."

"Okay. Let's talk next week." That was my unstated deal. I wouldn't jump the gun if she'd keep me in her world. It was a risk that I very well could have paid for with my career.

"Sounds good. Thanks." There was a touch more warmth in her voice.

A month later, the most terrible and beautiful day in my relationship with Kim came when I saw her walking down the hallway. Her eyes said that something was very wrong. She stood up artificially straight. Her smooth walk was forced. Her face was pressed into a calm that made me shudder. I couldn't say much for fear that she would shut me out. I just said a quiet hi and guided her gently to my office.

As soon as the door was closed and she was turned away from the glass, she looked up at me with a face that shredded my guts.

"I can't do this anymore. I'm in so much pain."

"What hurts?"

"My ribs. Please, it's fine. I just am so tired. I can't . . . "

She was openly crying. She hated crying. I knew she had to be in incredible pain.

"Just lay down in my office and take a rest. I'll come check on you later."

"Okay. Thanks." She looked at me, wondering if I would report this.

"It will be okay."

I wasn't sure what to do next, but I knew a line had been crossed. I needed to get more information if she would be willing to share it, and I knew this would have to be called in. But now was not the time. She had to rest. We had to talk.

I came back to check on her between meetings at other locations. I let her rest for a couple of classes, and then she seemed ready to finish her day. I contacted a chiropractor who might do some pro bono work, and he agreed to check her out.

Kim was pretty wiped out, so I let her go home without the heavy talk that was coming. The next day I told her that I had to report her situation to child welfare, and I invited her to make the call with me. This was the only way I could imagine where she wouldn't just deny the whole thing and make up very plausible cover stories.

"If I don't do this, I will likely get into trouble," I said.

"I don't want to get you in trouble, but I also don't want to make any more trouble for myself than I already have."

"I can only report what I know, and you haven't told me that anyone is hurting you, even though that's what I suspect. It's your choice to tell them whatever you wish, and even whether you want to identify yourself or not."

Kim stared at me intently. She made it clear that she cared about me; it would have been so easy for her to just walk away. I felt honored that she had let me past her formidable walls. She was also, very clearly, developing a plan.

We made the call, and the tension in the room was intense. Kim made it clear that she did not want me to identify her as I made the report. She sat near me, fidgeting and keeping her gaze fixed at the ground. The child welfare woman who spoke to me asked how I viewed the situation, and I told her what I had observed, wondering to myself if I would be asked to identify Kim. Should I overturn her decision if asked, because now was the time to get her some help? Should I honor her choice? I wasn't asked, so I let her choice stand. To my knowledge, child welfare did not follow up further on the call.

Some weeks later, on a day when I wasn't working, I heard that Kim came to school with a black eye. Child welfare was called to check it out, and they didn't do anything about it then as far as I could see. Kim explained to me later, "I told the child welfare lady that

I knew she needed me to confirm something was happening in order for her to be able to do anything about it, and that she wouldn't get a statement like that from me. Ever."

My difficult decisions were not over. In the weeks that followed, I felt that Kim was settling back into trying to pretend the impossible. "It's not that tough. Others are going through, and have gone through, way worse than me."

There were no clear injuries, but I wasn't sure if she was simply getting better at hiding them. In her hypothetical stories, she seemed to be standing up for someone in her life, taking the heat for them and paying for it. But there was still no disclosure that was reportable. I had to do something.

"I would like to call your parents and invite them to talk with me."

"Why would you want to do that?"

"I'm a glutton for punishment? I want to thank them for raising the most stubborn young woman on the planet?"

"You're a goof. Why, really?"

"Well, we haven't really talked about them much, but I think it's important since they're such a big part of your life. They'll get a chance to learn of my concern for you."

"We don't talk about them because there's never a need for me to bring them up. They're not involved enough in my life to make much of a difference. My dad works and my mom is retired army and too broken to really do much, which is why a lot of the stuff at home falls on me."

"What did your mom do in the army?"

"She was PSYOPs—basically, she did psychological warfare via propaganda in other countries."

"Hmm, psychological warfare? That explains what you've been putting me through this whole year." Kim smirked. "I think I need to look them in the eye and let them know that I'm concerned for their daughter."

I was sure she wouldn't go with my idea. She stared at me for a minute.

"Fine."

"Really?"

"Yeah."

I was sure they wouldn't come meet with us during the school day.

But they did.

I didn't know what to expect, but I definitely didn't expect what I saw. Kim's dad was grey haired, mellow, and short. He pulled Kim's mother's chair out for her. Kim's mom looked like she had been through some tough things, but she was clear-eyed, polite, and, of the two, the strongest. I chose my questions carefully and did not directly accuse or assume anything. Kim's mom did almost all the talking, and after small talk about their daughters and their work, I prepared to bring up some tidbit of my suspicion. Kim's mom was ready.

"I know what you're thinking," she said.

"I'm not sure what you mean."

"He is a gentle man. He's harmless. Look at him. He wouldn't do anything to anyone. If I wanted to, I could beat him up."

I was stunned. I felt like she was using psychological warfare on me . . . and it seemed to be working. I was confused. Her dad fit what she was saying; he kept looking down, only looking up at me briefly and meekly.

Kim's mom continued, "Now stop thinking this junk and let us be a family. We have a good family and we just want to love each other."

I had to look at Kim, who was sitting in the room, to get my bearings. She seemed like she was experiencing something she'd heard many times. She had no reaction. The whole thing was very bizarre. My gut was screaming, but it felt like someone had laid a blanket over it so I couldn't hear it clearly. I looked over at Kim's dad, and he still looked very meek. I didn't know what to do, so I said something about wanting to make sure that Kim was safe. I worried that they would somehow forbid her from talking to me. And then I let them go without doing anything that I had planned. On the way out, both parents hugged Kim and told her to have a good day.

When Kim's dad hugged her, I felt a wave of nausea that passed quickly. Both were polite as they said goodbye, but when Kim's mom looked into my eyes, I felt that she wished I was dead. After they left, I felt disoriented. I was relieved they were gone. I was mad at myself for perhaps wasting the only time when I might have pushed for the truth from them. I wanted to talk with Kim.

"That's how my mom is all the time. In the land she lives in, we're happy all the time."

"What about your dad?"

She looked at me as if to say, *Don't be dumb, Eric.*

"I have to say, that was one strange experience."

"It was your idea," she said with big, innocent eyes.

"Thanks. You're a big help."

Though it seemed like the meeting with her parents went no-where, Kim started to tell me more in her "hypothetical" stories. Indirectly, she let me see that her dad was beating her severely on a regular basis. She let me know that he believed women should be submissive and compliant, and that whenever Kim refused to follow his way, he was just giving her "what she deserved" because of her "disrespect." Kim seemed to half-believe this was the way he should be.

She later divulged that it was imperative to create her theory on emotions, because if she hadn't convinced herself that she could simply choose to be happy, she wouldn't have survived staying at home as long as she had.

She also began letting me know that she stayed largely for her mother and sister. She was scared about what would happen to her sister if she left, because she knew that if something did happen, her sister might act like her mother and cover the whole thing up. I tried many different ways to convince her to move out of the house and stay with friends. She resisted. She tried some of her old tricks, claiming that she could handle it, but she knew that I knew better.

The only thing that seemed to make a difference was when I said,

"I don't think you will ever truly be able to help your sister until you focus on getting yourself strong enough to help her see things as they really are. No one's parents should physically harm them. That is never good discipline, especially for a teenager."

Somehow, she finally decided to live with a friend. It turns out that she only stayed with her friend for a week before going back home. Her mother had made an agreement with Kim that if she came and spoke with her at the house, then she would be allowed to go back to her friend. But once the discussion was completed, Kim was locked in her bedroom and forced to stay home.

It wasn't until halfway through her senior year that Kim was able move out again, after she drove herself to a clinic because of shoulder and rib pain. While there, the doctor had told her rather bluntly that if she had hit the ground any harder, she would have shattered her collar bone.

Shortly after this incident, Kim and I had a long conversation in my office. She was in physical pain again, and she admitted to struggling with "her duty" as a daughter and as a sister. But after the inner torment of telling the truth, she was surprised to hear a very new kind of statement tumble out of her mouth: "I don't deserve to get hit!"

It surprised us both to hear it. I asked her to repeat the statement on multiple occasions so it would stop being awkward and start being solid truth.

Her senior year was filled with waves of guilt for betraying her family, but eventually she graduated and got a job out of state.

As I worked on this story with Kim, she reflected on the

experience. "Do I still regret leaving my sister? Yeah . . . but I don't think I'd be alive today if I hadn't. You helped me realize that putting my needs first isn't selfish, but necessary. You spoke to me like we were two adults having a conversation. I never got the embarrassing feeling that you felt pity for me, but instead that you legitimately cared, which for me was a new sensation.

"One of the best things you did for me was help me feel confident in my ability to talk to you without the fear of potential repercussions from 'the system.' You were someone I could bounce ideas and theories off of, and not get the feeling that you were just another adult looking at me either like a problem child or as just some needy kid. Yeah, I needed help, but I needed to help myself and not have someone else do it for me. You gave me the mental tools to understand that my shitty situation was actually tearing away my humanity."

We laughed about the fact that she was reading the story we had written about her with her *fiancé* ("Never get married, hmmm?"). She invited me to officiate her wedding, and I got to watch Kim struggle with whether to allow her dad to participate. She finally allowed him to do so, and it was a beautiful, redemptive expression of that part of her story.

Less than a year later, I received a texted picture of a white plastic device with the caption "pregnant."

EMOTIONS DON'T EXIST—ANALYSIS

SUMMARY

A rational young woman creates a life philosophy that allows her to deny her emotions in order to endure emotional, mental, physical, and spiritual abuse while remaining loyal to her family.

THE TRAP

"I have tension between what my emotions are doing and what my family needs me to do. I create a system that seems to work, but something about it is false, and I hate falseness. I go to great lengths to hide my suffering and protect my broken family. In my commitment to do so, I often believe my father is right: that I am the problem, that I bring punishment on myself because I have been 'disrespectful' by questioning my family's way. My mother's frequent comments that 'nothing is happening' also seem correct to me. Breaking these perceptions is incredibly hard because I often can't see outside of them. Wrecking my constructed reality comes with a heavy price. I have built a system to keep my family together. It cannot fail."

THE WAY OUT

In order to respectfully get past Kim's walls, I had to keep returning to two principles:

Know Thy Other

- Don't disrupt people without seeing how they fit into their world (perception).

- People have good reasons for the patterns they create (even if they contain destructive elements).

Home Dirt, Healthy Plant

- Help people where they are, with what they have.

- A good *fit* is one of the most important elements of true help.

★

ROCKY MOUNTAIN PUB, COLORADO

The location for the interview with Psyche is in an informal conference room in the back of a pub in Coronado, Colorado, about an hour from my office. Cecillia, acting more like an agent than an editor, thought it would be a good way to get some early connections to promote the book. She pushed me to do it because she knows I'm stuck in the writing process and hopes this will get me "to the finish line." I feel like she's making me present my thoughts with my pants half-on.

The drive to the pub is full of steep, winding roads and corners, which open up to beautiful views of the snow-capped Rockies. I arrive at the pub, park, and enter through the large, wooden barn doors. The bartender points me to a door behind the bar when I ask about the conference room. Inside I find a rough-hewn table, five heavy wooden chairs, and one sharp-eyed, dark-haired woman in her thirties waiting for me. I get the sense that this is not Cecillia's friend, Janelle, who was interested in reciprocal dignity. The mysterious woman smiles, shakes my hand, and gestures for me to sit without saying a word.

In the few seconds of silence, I see on the table one of the summary pages I sent ahead that distills the first of the six stories down to some core elements to help guide our discussion…

The interviewer does not tell me her name even after I tell her mine. She simply smiles and begins.

(***Interviewer***) Why did Kim trust you? Sometimes you seemed as much of a pain in her butt as she was in yours. You were another potentially controlling man who was messing with her protections.

(***Eric***) Well, you just jump right in don't you? Kim says the trust came from persistence and respect. I couldn't have faked either one with her watchful eye. She had to experience my seeing elements in her that I truly admired and cherished. And you're right that I had to be careful when I challenged her protections, even if they kept her suffering going.

(***Interviewer***) I can see how you could respect her, because she's fascinating in many ways, but what about someone who is less intelligent or interesting? How do you want to *Know Thy Other* if you don't find them interesting?

(***Eric***) That's tricky, and a similar challenge is on the flip side of that coin—what to do when I find someone very interesting. With Kim, I wasn't sure if what I enjoyed was okay. I liked the challenge of breaking through her defenses. She drew out my love of strategy games: I had to be strategic every time I met with her. I had to think ahead about how my words or actions might affect her and what was truly best for the whole situation, not just the immediate issue. Was there something wrong with me that I enjoyed it? Wouldn't it be more respectful to let her have her walls and let her choose her own path or somehow be neutral about her? Was I deciding that my way was better than hers?

Your question is also important because I struggle the most when I feel like anyone could help this person and I am not needed. I'm troubled by the idea that my being bored with one person's burdens might prove that I think I am too good for their situation.

What I have come to realize is that whatever I feel when I'm meeting with someone, even if it's strong or negative, I can use it to build *reciprocal dignity*. I am not using the people I meet with to build my private strategic capacity; rather I am learning with them and being interested in them. The connection and mutuality make the difference.

I have had to work to develop a game I call Infinite Curiosity so that if my initial experience is one of boredom, lethargy, or separation, then I can get past it. It's an in-my-head game where I pursue some element inside a person which reveals their uniqueness. Sometimes I have to almost trick myself into forgetting that initial impression so I can keep openly pursuing the person. I've often found that the "bad" initial experience was not the real person in front of me; it's just that they've hidden beneath an unattractive protective layer (e.g. boring/lethargic to lower expectations and pressure). I have to honor my initial sense and let it teach me, but also I have to not let it rule the relationship. Respect naturally follows when I see people deeply and when my actions are in accordance with their best qualities and in tune with what their weaknesses can teach me. This allows the *Know Thy Other* practice to function.

(*Interviewer*) Okay, so this reminds me that you're trying to show how this different method of "counseling" has changed *you*. What did Kim teach you about *Home Dirt, Healthy Plant?* And also, you never said what her philosophy on emotions has become...

(*Eric*) Oops. You're right. When I asked Kim about her current philosophy of emotions, she said, "They're very important, sometimes scary and hard." She's pretty efficient with her words. She is allowing herself to be loved and to feel what she didn't think she could, and that is fabulous to me.

One critical lesson that came out of my experiences with Kim was learning how to facilitate respectful movement away from old patterns that had worked in the past, but now cause problems. We had to wade into Kim's self-denying philosophy together first. When she saw how her system hurt her relationship with me and didn't work in other ways, she allowed herself to imagine a new way. She had to see her own value more clearly, to imagine better ways to protect or strengthen her family, before she could begin trying to step out of her broken patterns. Doing so too early would likely have led to harm.

(*Interviewer*) How do you use this *Home Dirt* but also provoke enough new "fertilization" or change to step into being a new *Healthy Plant?*

(*Eric*) I interviewed many people asking what helped them break out of their inner traps, and I had to laugh when about half of them said, "You got in the way and stopped me," while the other half said, "You got out of the way and let me do it." Both are called for in different circumstances, but discerning how and when to do either one is not easy. It tends to become clearer when I have a sense of what shapes their "home dirt." A friend calls this process "determining their currency": Unless I know what is available to grow in or what they use to give and receive with others, I won't know if the priority is to stop them (e.g. finding the exceptions in their system) or make room for them (e.g. create a safe frame for them to create within).

For Kim this began with an understanding that she was not familiar with trust. She didn't have it for herself, her family, or really anyone. So the question became, "How do I create the conditions for Kim to begin enjoying some small tastes of good trust?" Our philosophy game honored her need to play it safe, and it also made room for her to push her own limits and try another way.

(*Interviewer*) Many organizations are not flexible enough to discover elements you pursued with *Know Thy Other*, or discovering what made her *Home Dirt* function. Were you bending the rules to work with Kim the way you did?

(*Eric*) That is a hard question. In general, no. I usually feel comfortable being creative within the rules; however, there are times when a rule and what is best for the person seem to conflict. In those situations, I try to honor both sides as best I can. In Kim's story, when to report initial suspicions of abuse was a very hard "rule" to know how to apply in her best interest. As a highly intuitive person, I could report suspicion very early with no evidence and likely sever many relationships. Is this what should be done? How should I know when to report if not at first sign?

It is additionally challenging when supportive organizations are under-resourced or stressed. The school mental health team I worked under had to operate within systems that were not always dependable. Human service agencies, particularly in rural communities, are often underfunded and overworked. Good people stretched to their limits have a hard time being flexible. When a thin thread of trust is at risk, it is hard to believe a call to CPS (Child Protective Services) in our area would be handled sensitively even if the evidence is very clear.

(*Interviewer*) I don't think you are answering my question directly enough. I will ask it a different way: Is there anything that can be done so that you or people like you don't end up in bad positions like that? How can you honor a person's *Home Dirt* when an organization requires a client to function within their system's rules in order to get support?

(*Eric*) In my experience, organizational systems that are not designed to prepare and support staff for these situations contribute to "bad positions." The people on the front line have to be ready to handle the risks of uncertainty when the standard protocols aren't enough. Learning *discernment* is an often neglected aspect of wisdom—to see the hidden possibilities beyond the immediate ones and choose the best course of action. Finding what would be "salt" for one person (to make them thirsty for more good) may be completely different for another person.

This often begins with admitting that we professionals actually know very little about any person we meet with. We are dependent on what we are told, and often a great deal remains unseen. For example, meeting Kim's parents that one time taught me far more than the many conversations Kim and I had about them.

(*Interviewer*) Can the principle of *Home Dirt, Healthy Plant* be applied to organizations?

(*Eric*) It can, because *Home Dirt* is essentially culture. Organizations have culture, and when they are intentional about cultivating it, they have more fertile dirt to work with. However, in the early stages of culture development, new insights can come that are challenging to deal with.

Once, in a rare collaborative initiative between our school mental health team, a high school, and CPS, information was shared about a young lady who reported ongoing sexual abuse from her father. CPS had determined on nine previous instances, due to a fabricated psych evaluation of the young lady by her parents, that she was a pathological liar and her reports of abuse were false. For a decade, this brave young woman risked harm from her family in order to get help. Instead she was blamed by nearly everyone involved. When we discovered this rationale for inaction, we informed the CPS representative that there was zero evidence of pathological lying at school and that she did show signs of covering up abuse to avoid scrutiny. This time CPS reacted swiftly, but without helping the young lady prepare. She was taken out of her home and placed with an ill-equipped foster family who didn't know how to support her when her biological family disowned and threatened her. She lost what few supports she had, got involved in a bad romantic relationship, and ended up raising a child alone. I last saw her working hard at a restaurant, trying to piece her life together.

School had been her haven, and she had frequently been seen skipping down the hallways with a beaming smile. She worked extremely hard in her classes. No one guessed the horrors she faced at home. This should not have happened to her. Building her existing supports and developing new ones could have really helped her when the truth came out.

So often, funding and certification requirements shape organizations more than their own cultural wisdom. This tends to make the organizations vulnerable when major changes occur. I have a good friend who works in the child protection system and he works very hard to interview young people in order to find truth and justice for each situation. He has shown me how challenging this task can be when so many factors push an employee in these extreme circumstances to harden up or become jaded just to survive what is witnessed.

Workers like him need our support, and they need people to be a part of the identification and recovery process so that the professionals and the children have good care. To find new ways to do this, the people I worked with were sometimes required to take some big steps outside the established norms—this was risky, but the valuable lessons were important to me.

(*Interviewer*) You mention in your summary that "a good fit" is one of the most important aspects of good help. What do you mean?

(*Eric*) Counselors tend to be trained around exemplars, models, and practices. There are business pressures to become an "expert" on these elements and to use them to attract referrals or clients. It then becomes easy to paste these favorite modes onto anyone who will receive them. This is not what a good fit means. The counselors I have most respected have acquired versatile humility and insight into how to set up the space and conditions around a person so that they will flourish. This often requires the counselor to learn and change as much as the client. One family recently guided me to first meet their son at a smoothie shop for fifteen minutes outdoors with one parent present. The second meeting was set up in another informal location. We spoke about how other people had overcome similar struggles without mentioning the son's struggles, or even what my job was. It was critical to avoid words that sounded medical or at all related to mental health, because that would shut down the conversation and the relationship. I had to adapt in many ways to the son, or we wouldn't even get to start. I had to learn a great deal or I would likely unintentionally ruin the relationship and have no idea what happened. This required a lot of preliminary work with the parents and an understanding of the son's history before I jumped into any talk of solutions or methods.

(*Interviewer*) How do you handle long-term situations where there is no resolution at the end and the problems keep going on?

(*Eric*) Let's let the next story address that question. Sarah is like many women I have known who, with a twisted compassion, hurt themselves to protect others. It was hard to resolve because it was good which has been attached to a dark anchor: Sarah developed a friendship with an entity she named Evil.

As the interviewer stands to exit, she pauses, and then pulls a small slip of paper out of her pocket and slides it toward me. There is only a sketch on the paper:

As I look at it, the eye pierces me—it makes me feel opened up, known, unprotected. I look back at the woman. Is this a break? She wasn't talking with me very long. Did I do a good job so far? This doesn't seem like the typical interview process for a book, but I am fairly new at this and not sure what to do. She leaves, and because I don't know her name I decide to call her Ebony (after her hair color).

I look back down at the paper. The eye intrigues and bothers me. I am drawn to it, and yet it makes me feel uneasy.

Is that what my clients feel when I understand them a little too quickly?

Is this what I might feel if I were deeply seen?

Dear reader,

Reciprocal dignity is a simple-sounding idea that is rarely applied in Western cultures, so it is easy to miss when it starts to appear.

It is also easy to step on the dignity of another person, even with good intentions. But this danger does not mean we must be hyper-protective.

We tend to offer advice and tidy solutions when what is needed instead is a patient, receptive ear; to understand requires us to be open to being changed.

This does not mean we have nothing to offer, or that our advice is worthless. It does mean that what we have needs to be molded into a shape that fits the other before it is given, or it is unlikely to stick. Something in us needs to be receptive and flexible before we can help. Often this requires letting go of the intention to be "helpful."

Father Gregory Boyle of the Homeboy Industries gang intervention network refers to this as "going to the margins and allowing yourself to be reached."

In the next story, watch for ways in which Sarah brings her existing strengths and current awareness of reality to me. Notice also how it helps me create new things with her. At times, this means our relationship has to change; the rules of relating have to shift. Sometimes my eyes have to open in a new way, and at other times hers must.

I will once again use a variety of forms to give you experiences that might resonate with you—a poetic introduction, a story of two people, an image, and two wisdom principles analyzed. If one of these doesn't work for you, move on. The variety increases the odds of connection, but most people aren't wired to receive them all.

E

Hundreds of people can talk for one who can think,
but thousands can think for one who can see.
To see clearly is poetry, prophecy, and religion — all in one.
— *John Ruskin*

III

FRIENDS WITH EVIL

A Dream of Wise Counsel
  I see the valleys and valleys filled with bondage;
  They converse and confirm – so many empty nods and smiles;
  They swim in lethargic waters – rippling in one ongoing, pulsing
      pattern –
  They do not travel, only move.

(Eric) I was working late at a small high school and felt tired. My office was near a large section of lockers and I took a break, leaning against them to watch the few students and adults still on campus after hours. I was lost in thought when I noticed a young lady named Sarah walking toward me. She seemed to me like a child stumbling out of a dark fog—beaten down, but working hard to connect.

(*Sarah*) Being part of the theatre, I often stayed late at school. On one of those days, I looked down the hallway and saw Eric.

"Go."

A strange voice spoke to me from nowhere and everywhere. I was scared. Was I going crazy? But it seemed like a good voice, and it wanted me to talk with Eric. I always saw him around school helping people, but I was used to a different voice telling me, "You shouldn't get help. See how far you can fall. It feels good being a nothing. It's who you are. No one knows. It's your thing. Your secret. Your security."

I couldn't let go of that . . . it was all I had! I didn't trust anything to be better, because what if I got my hopes up and it turned out worse?

I heard it again. "Go."

Scary as it felt, I had to talk with Eric because now I was hearing voices.

One of the ways our Community Advocates program at the school got to know students in a less clinical way was to accompany them on field trips and share daily activities, like lunch, without an agenda. On one occasion, I had driven art students, including Sarah, to visit a series of art colleges and had been dubbed "Captain Eric" by my passengers. Perhaps this helped my initial connection to Sarah, because during our first meeting she jumped straight into sharing the deep waters of her mind and heart as if she had known and trusted me her entire life. I didn't understand how she could open up so quickly, and it scared me a little—I didn't want to mishandle such tenderness. I also noticed she tended to wear long sleeve shirts even when the weather was warm—could be a fashion choice, or that she wants to hide her arms. My "be careful" sense was alerting me.

From a very young age, I felt isolated. There was something keeping me from connecting with other children my age. I was the ugly duckling of my group of friends. I didn't look the way they looked: I wasn't petite or cute or graceful or delicate. I was the opposite of all that, chunky and dorky and clumsy and a host of other not-cute things.

Because of all this, I was bullied. But the insults that hurt the worst were the ones directed at my brother. My brother has autism, and back when we were kids, he was very energetic and usually unaware of the odd things he sometimes did. When out at recess, I remember always having to keep an eye on him to make sure nothing would break his bubble of innocence and joy.

My brother needed my attention at home, too. There, it seemed so much of our lives was centered on him. He needed extra nurturing, so my parents gave everything they could to him. I stayed quiet and tried to not stir up any trouble so I wouldn't add to their stress. But when I did, the guilt would send me into a deep depression.

My parents didn't understand my need for gentleness and depth. This made me feel like I was born into the wrong family. Maybe they needed a child who wouldn't cause them so much stress and would appreciate what they could give instead of feeling starved and left out by it. My parents seemed to be always on edge, and the person I was starting to grow into was more independent and talked back sometimes—something they weren't used to. They often overreacted, trying to make me change. When their reactions hurt me, they called me "overly sensitive." They wouldn't ever hurt me physically, but my heart felt crushed, especially when they'd attack my personality. They hadn't been able to get to know me, and in not knowing me, they didn't know how to love or punish me.

After many misunderstood attempts over the years to hint at what was going on with me, I hardened into what I already felt: that it was better to not tell them anything.

As time went on, I started feeling drawn to darker things. It freaked me out a little, so I began reading the Bible, hoping to protect myself. The anxiety of disappointing my parents and wanting to avoid another incident made me decide I needed to get baptized as insurance against guilt, failure, and the calling darkness. After telling my dad about wanting to be baptized, he said he wanted to perform it in the backyard pool. We weren't part of a church, so that seemed just fine. Maybe this would get rid of my increasing feelings of numbness and nothingness, too!

Well, I was dunked and lifted out of the water feeling . . . nothing. No love. No joy. Nothing. I expected awesomeness, freedom, connection with God, and I didn't get any of it. It seemed like a forgettable moment.

As I wondered what I could have done wrong, my brother decided he wanted to be baptized too, right then! He waded over to my dad with all of his innocent goofiness and splashed my dad to get his attention. I just stood there stunned. *Do you even know what this is about?* I thought. *This is supposed to be my moment with Jesus and I can't even have that.*

Watching my dad baptize my brother filled me with anger and resentment. I tried to take hold of my mind, shocked by my hateful feelings not even two minutes after making a public display of love for Jesus. Maybe I still wasn't saved after all? Maybe I needed to earn God's love, prove to Jesus I really did love him, hoping that He would forgive me for having a tainted baptism.

But it only got worse when I reached high school. My inability to really connect with people made me feel so isolated. I wanted to be graceful and tender and gently nurturing like the images of good feminine figures I read about in the Bible, but there were parts of me that didn't fit that image. I wanted to die and had horrible images of violence frequently in my head. It didn't feel feminine or right to see these things. It felt shameful. But after a while, these "differences" became part of who I thought I was, a person I would never let anyone know existed.

I became so used to feeling like a hollow waste of life that I was sort of addicted to it. I couldn't live without it. It was comforting to rest in the belief that I was evil and worthless. Maybe then I could stop trying to be perfect and failing.

Then came the day the voice told me to meet with you, Eric. That first time I talked to you, it was non-stop. Everything just poured out. You just sat there listening. It felt like a dam had broken, and I was addicted to the releasing pressure. It felt so good and freeing. I could do this all day. This was a safe place. I faked who I was all the time to survive, even to myself, but maybe I didn't have to anymore.

About the third time we talked, you began asking me questions about who I was inside. It felt amazing—the best time of my life! No one else had ever showed that kind of interest in me, and I didn't feel so alone in the world anymore.

You couldn't believe there was any part of you that was good; it was a very painful experience, and I felt it. Your trust, your heart, and your tenderness all touched me, and when you bashed on yourself, I felt like I was witnessing bullying. How could I show you how I saw you?

I attempted a Strengths Tree exercise where you filled in leaves on the tree with your good qualities, hoping the visual would appeal to your artistic mind. But you could only do a couple leaves before trying to scratch them out.

I hated that tree. Just looking at it made me want to destroy it. I'm ugly—I inherited my dad's looks and they don't work for a woman. I'm a mess inside too. I couldn't believe that anyone would care about me once they knew how I really was.

You tried lots of things, but they didn't make it to my heart. There was only one thing that convinced me you really cared: when I saw you get angry for the first time.

I had a good friend at school who was going through his own set of problems and he did hard drugs to deal with it. I thought that might work for me too—trying to think better of myself was too scary, so I decided to fall apart instead, knowing that taking that path could lead to my destruction.

My friend knew where to buy cocaine and was willing to help me get some. Well, you somehow found out. I've seen my parents get angry, but I had never seen the kind of anger you had. My friend and I were standing in the common area talking about cocaine when you walked up with fire in your eyes and a hint of disappointment on your face. You told my friend, "You will not, under any circumstances, help her get drugs!" Your tone stunned me, not with fear but with the realness of it. It was real concern you had—real! Being a calm and completely collected counselor wasn't the answer in that moment, and that's when I knew you cared. You didn't care because you were paid to, you cared because you were my friend.

After a few weeks of meeting together off and on, Sarah's mother, who worked at the school, said she was uncomfortable with Sarah seeing me if it meant missing classes. Sarah had not used cocaine after my confrontation, but my suspicion that Sarah's long sleeves were covering self-harm had been growing, and it was nearing time to report it. I needed to handle this with care because I didn't want to damage Sarah's trust—she didn't have anyone else she would go to for help.

When she finally admitted to cutting herself a number of times, I asked Sarah's permission to talk with her parents about the temptation to hurt herself so that neither of us would be in trouble down the road. Sarah's body language said, "Don't make me do this." But in the end, with considerable reluctance, she agreed to let me talk with her dad. It was a risk for both of us.

When her big, stressed-out dad came into my office, he appeared braced for bad news and ready to fight. I imagined how it might feel if I went to see an unknown counselor who knew something bad about my daughter that I didn't. Not fun. Though I tried to offer a tone of understanding, it was clear that he was not happy that I "had known" she'd been cutting herself but hadn't told him earlier.

Sarah later said that her parents were angry and didn't believe I was handling the situation well, so they hired an outside therapist to help.

The therapist my parents had found was nice and kind, but I knew after my experience with my parents finding out too much about me that I needed to conceal and stay closed off. I told her only what my parents already knew from the meeting with Eric. After only a few months of therapy, my parents asked me if I felt better, and of course I said yes, telling them what I knew would make *them* feel better. The therapy was, to me, a waste of time. Yes, it was nice to be able to chit-chat about life, but there was no true connection or challenge. Traditional therapy was like that—it felt very "by the book" and practiced.

After it became clear her new counselor wasn't really helping, I was allowed to meet with Sarah again. I needed to understand the roots of her desire to hurt herself. The more I learned, the deeper and earlier in life the pattern seemed to have been formed. I wondered if we would be able to find a way to break it without breaking Sarah.

Although Sarah trusted me, there were things she didn't want to talk about. Her interest in dark artwork and music grew and she incorporated more of it into her identity. Early in her high school years, she was drawn to zombies, blood and gore, and grunge clothing. As she got older, her interests grew darker. She surrounded herself with people who were interested in the same things. I couldn't fully understand this war that seemed to be deepening within Sarah, so one day, as a guess, I asked, "What kind of guys are you attracted to?"

They are all into the same darkness I am.

Why are you attracted to that?

It makes the guys mysterious, but also familiar. I get a weird little family dynamic out of hanging out with them, and it feels good to not be alone. These guys say the thoughts I'm afraid to speak out loud. Listening to them talk is comforting, even though they have lots of problems.

It seems like you like it and struggle with it at the same time.

It makes me wonder, "Why am I the only girl who seems to be captivated by this?" Being surrounded by guys made me miss having girlfriends. I found a few female friends who would deal with me for a little while, but it always ended with me feeling like a burden. So I'd slowly distance myself and leave.

Sarah, do you see how you tend to be drawn to people and things that keep you held back? Even when you're in a relationship, you get left out.

It's what I am used to. Other people matter more than me. I started cutting to feel something other than all the chaos. I want so badly to kill the parts of myself that make me feel isolated. With cutting, I can punish myself and have a couple days of being able to act like everything is okay. The more time goes on, the shorter and shorter the cycle becomes. It allows me to punish myself, get some relief, hate myself, and feel some clear pain—and after it's done, I do something wrong or feel shame, which builds up, and I want to do it again . . . soon.

Sometimes what builds up inside me is the feeling of overwhelming injustice. I am so infuriated by the evil done to others by people. The thought that people can be so cruel to one another and keep living their lives makes my soul ache. The hatred I had for sin developed into a love-hate relationship with being human. The thought that I was part of the problem consumed my soul! "God why did you give me life? How could you! I don't want to be here with all of this evil and feel it all!" I couldn't cope with being alive, and as punishment for being alive I needed to hurt myself as much as I could while I was here.

I see how justice is important to you, but it doesn't really seem like true justice if you are constantly beat up. It seems like you are numb because you are overwhelmed and sad about not being understood or getting what you need. The more you tell me about your life, the more it seems there are other reasons why that happens—not that you are such a hard person to understand or love.

I know that my parents had their own struggles that made my situation hard for them. When my problems were brought to light and I became more visibly troubled, my mom wasn't able to relate or cope. For her well-being, she asked my dad to become my main parent.

My boyfriend, Max, confronted me one day because I had cut "loser" into my leg. He said, "I am not going to date someone like that. It's immature. You need to figure out a way to deal with your emotions other than this. I can't be with someone who can't handle themselves."

It kind of blew my mind. "Who do you think you are?!" I asked him at the time. But somehow it got through to me. Max started to symbolize that I could be better. He would tell me, "You could be someone who changes people and the world. Be someone who believes they matter!" I even started to believe my art could affect people.

I saw a future for us. He challenged me to be better. I wanted to see where it would lead. I wanted to have a reason to stop cutting. I couldn't stop for my parents, my brother, myself, or God. But this was an opportunity for something new. It was the ultimatum that I needed. I still thought about cutting, but my need for love trumped my need to hurt myself.

Sarah graduated from high school, and that technically was supposed to be the end of our "counseling." I was working for a school-based mental health program and she was out of school . . . simple! Of course not. Adult responsibilities came fast and were very challenging for her to navigate. There was so much more for us to talk about, but standard practice was for clear separation at transition times. Sarah was looking for a job where she could help people, and I hoped that I would be able to indirectly support her.

I got a job at a residential treatment center to help misfits like me. It didn't help my depression—I was often sad because I couldn't do what was right. I couldn't have a relationship with the clients like the one you had with me. "Professional boundaries" and medical rules prevented it. It seemed so shallow to think that you could join with someone, help them, and then let them go so quickly and easily, which is common at a treatment center. I knew the residents better than I knew my "friends" because I was with them forty hours a week. I wanted so badly for them to know me so they would let me know them.

There was a funny day when some residents at the center asked me, "Why don't you live with us here? You're crazier than we are." Being told you're crazy by a bunch of institutionalized teenagers might offend some, but that was one of the sweetest, most genuine things anyone's ever said to me. I felt truly at home whenever I was with them.

I had been heavily trained and had good opportunities being a Peer Support Specialist, but I was young and overloaded with too many meetings, expectations, and bosses. I felt used by the adults who wanted a look into the minds of the youth. I was spread too thin. They would say, "I forget that sometimes you have problems, too." We told ourselves to "help them where they're at," but we didn't apply that to staff, so I burned out. It was devastating.

I was lost and it became clear that the job was harming me. I tried to find something else to help me, like my faith, but there was something missing in it that I couldn't see. I wished all the suffering could come onto me and not onto anyone else.

When Sarah told me about her experiences at the mental health center, it made me very sad. Family and friends had called Sarah "too sensitive," "overdramatic," or "too soft-hearted," and her needs were not understood. "Just stop making everything such a big deal!" was the message that kept coming at her.

I wanted to yell out, "Sensitivity is the capacity to sense vital elements in life!" What is being "soft" but the capacity to feel and care, to be affected and connected? These strengths can be overwhelming, but they remain strengths if protections and discernment are learned. Sarah couldn't stop being the way she was, but being misunderstood made her feel unfixable" and "stupid."

I have the same potential to be overwhelmed. When my observing eyes, analytical mind, and sensing heart are all operating together, I can take in more than I can handle. As a boy, if my emotions revealed that I was heavily affected by something, my peers would often send the message to "toughen up" because it wasn't "manly" to be like that. It was hard to learn not to hide my emotions, but to allow them to teach me without controlling me. I hoped that I helped Sarah learn the same.

One of my darker girlfriends who lived with me pressured me to smoke pot, and she constantly exposed everyone to immoral art and entertainment. She brought home lots of guys and drugs. She treated my boyfriend—now my husband—and me like parents who would let her do anything. I was too compassionate with her, because I knew the evil in her was similar to mine. It all felt tainted and wrong, like we were all being drawn further into darkness.

My husband saw I was falling apart and kicked my friend out after we got married. He had to stop it for my protection. Protection is what I always needed but couldn't get. We had to move if there was to be any hope of change, so we moved out of state to put distance between us and our past. A couple months later, we found out I was pregnant. I couldn't believe it; I was so angry at God. "You know what I am going through, and you give me a kid!" I sank into a ditch of nothingness. I started to experience chaos in my mind to a degree I never had before. Even breastfeeding felt like it would tear me apart. I was warring with myself to the point of contemplating suicide.

We moved back to our old hometown, which was a relief, but also stressful at the same time. The familiar things were both refreshing and scary—the reminders of the dark times in my life were right nearby. We found a great deal on a cute house, but it was right across the street from my old high school. Darkness had lived in me there, and my body and mind reminded me of it.

When I spoke with Sarah after she moved back, it was like she wasn't fully there. She has a brightness to her even when she is suffering, but now it was hard to see or sense. I could tell she carried an impossible burden on her shoulders, but she refused to put it down. She seemed to want to die slowly and painfully no matter what I did. I didn't have an official place in her life anymore, and it made me wonder if she actually wanted me to keep connecting with her.

I hadn't talked with Sarah for a long time, until one day I felt it was important to call her. I didn't know why. She didn't respond, but I felt compelled to keep trying.

For two months I didn't contact you even though you kept trying to reach me. I wanted to hurt myself and die, but it was in the background. I didn't want to be reminded of it. I felt like if I talked with you, I would have to come face to face with it. So I did what I do best: I withdrew and hid. I tried to shield everyone from my inner storm.

It didn't work. After many meltdowns, I pushed myself to reach out and try to create what my husband and I hoped for when we moved here—friends and good relationships. We started hanging out with some old friends who had also been through hard stuff. It was so refreshing but also felt so fragile—I was afraid I would ruin it. Like when I had a frank talk with an old friend about my struggles, and I felt so bad afterward because I thought she might go away. I didn't want her to see me as someone who was too dark. Thankfully I saw that she was feeling what I felt! Maybe it wasn't to the same degree, but the chaos was there, the anxiety was there; the bad days happened for her, too. Having people in my life walking the same journey gives me the sense of fellowship that I desperately need. The healing that comes from genuine friendship is beautiful. It made me realize that there was more to my relationship with darkness, and I needed to talk about it if I was going to really heal.

Sarah agreed to let me interview her for this book. We talked about her story, and there was something that seemed to be blocking her movement forward. Despite successes she had experienced, like learning to trust and growing in her relationship with her husband, she seemed to be holding onto something that kept her from fully healing. My first clue came when she spoke to me about her cutting, and a look came onto her face like yearning for a lost love.

I need to tell you something that I was scared to talk about when I was younger.

Once, when I was sixteen years old, I was cutting myself with a razor blade when I became suddenly aware of something with me in the darkness. I felt it so strongly—like seeing something or hearing an audible voice, but with a different kind of sense. It was familiar, as if it had always been there. I was suddenly filled with memories that made me realize how long *it* had been with me. When I was little and sad, *it* was there. When I was bullied and lonely, I felt *him*, just as I do now.

I remember when I was seven, we had kids with disabilities around our house because of my mom's type of work. There was a boy, Thomas, who was around twelve but had the mental maturity of a one-year-old. He drooled and was in a walker. I had nightmares about him. I was uncomfortable being around him and didn't want him to touch me. I felt horrible. I wanted so badly to be compassionate and kind, but all the emotions and fear made me unable to. Going back, the evil presence was there, telling me how horrible I was for feeling this way towards someone so much in need of love.

I had always thought this presence was a part of me—I thought maybe I was just a worse person than most, or that I was just being "overly sensitive." But after I realized how long *it* had been with me, I welcomed *it* in more. *It* became more tangible, an old friend. Before, I thought I was evil and that the things I did were evil. After I realized it was *this thing* the whole time, I still felt evil, but now I wasn't alone. It felt spiritual. Hurting myself physically became something dear to my heart. Thinking about it still makes my mouth taste like copper and my body ache like I'm having withdrawals. It was like a twisted form of worship.

I have seen you like that, and it shook me to see it. I felt like your ability to love was somehow being spent on something that was very bad for you, but you were deeply attached to it anyway. Didn't it scare you to have some entity like that in your life?

It didn't scare me because *it* felt so familiar, so comforting. I could say, "So what if I'm crazy?" because I finally felt okay with how people always made me feel. I was evil, and Evil was *with* me. This evil made me know that *it* was like me, so I was not alone. I was in constant "prayer" with *it*. I talked with *it* in my head and it made me feel comforted, like it was okay that I was a horrible person.

It makes sense to me now why you were so resistant to anything good being connected to you in high school. If you allowed that to happen, you would lose the little that kept you going. It reminds me of people I have known who have been in abusive relationships where their partner degraded them so much that they became dependent on the partner for everything. It also seems like it took some pressure off you to be "bad."

It felt so good to not try so hard anymore—to be the person I thought I needed to be. I had felt a lot of pressure to be good and to make my parents proud; I wanted so badly to please them until I thought I might as well try stuff and not pretend to be good. So I planned on dying at eighteen, and I was just waiting out the clock.

It allowed me to be reckless, to want to try drugs, to try dating Max even though I didn't feel good enough for him. *Evil* didn't care as long as it didn't affect *its* role. *It* was okay with my marrying Max until it became clear that Max might make *it* have less of a part in my life. As long as I was being dark, *it* was fine. When I thought I could be better, that was the threat.

Later, being a mother wasn't enough to fight the voice of Evil. *It* told me, "Anyone can raise your daughter. You aren't important to the equation. Besides, how could someone like *you* love anyone?" *It* used my feelings and what people have told me against me. I let the voice continue because it was relaxing, made sense, mellowed me out, and it seemed a better reality.

As Sarah talked about her relationship with Evil, I was surprised to sense that her bond with him was already beginning to break. I said, "This is a confusing mix of good and bad things. You need less pressure. You need to understand yourself. You need to know your value, and Evil gave you some form of these things even though it held you hostage to get them. Does talking about this help you see the difference between what you really need and what you were given: a shadow of that need?

Now that so much time has passed I can finally see it all for what it was, a hollow image of the real thing. My needs are valid, and needing compassion and love is not wrong—it's normal and necessary for growth.

Seeing herself differently allowed Sarah to separate herself from Evil and from the things in life that overwhelmed her. It was not easy. Her little daughter, who shares Sarah's empathetic strengths, would often sense what was inside her mother and reflect back at her a magnified form of her feelings. This was like torture until Sarah understood what was happening. During a brief period where she felt better, some new questions arose.

Eric, now that I'm feeling better, I'm confused in a new way. Do you think this battle of mine is a psychological thing or a spiritual thing? Is Evil real?

If medication, physical remedies, or supportive people make a person "better," does that prove it was strictly a physiological or relational issue? Suffering people can have greater sensitivity and different awareness than when they suffer less. I have encountered too many people trapped by similar elements, attributed to something like Evil, to dismiss it as simply a fabrication or illusion.

Sarah had to work hard to break her need for the relationship with Evil because it was so old, familiar, and strong. She found that she needed discipline and mental practices to help her see and accept the good in her life.

I know I need to stop withdrawing and beating myself up. It's an old habit built on lies that I believed for most of my life. When you visit me I have to fight those lies, because when I look into your eyes, I can't deny that you care about me. I have to face that trap you set for me: to dismiss you as wrong or foolish for thinking well of me (which I can't do because I think you're smart), or agree with you and believe I am, maybe, a little beautiful. You showed me (hundreds of times) that I have rare gifts which can be used to help people, but that they must be trained.

I see a lot. I feel a lot. I care a lot. I want to stop wasting my energy by beating myself up for what I don't have. I want to learn to receive what I need so I am not always depleted, and so I have more to give. I need to be strong and healthy for my family and those I hope to serve when motherhood becomes less demanding. I want to use this time of motherhood to learn. I must allow myself to lean on others when I need to and allow them to lean on me when I can handle it. It still feels new and somewhat foreign. Sometimes it even feels wrong, like I can't handle the goodness or like it might go away and leave me even sadder.

Evil is still there on the outskirts of my life. *It* becomes more present in the moments where I can choose to turn to the old ways of thinking instead of choosing the new way. When I feel like a horrible person, *it* is an option. I'm sad to admit that it was comforting in the beginning to know *it* will be there if I invite *it* back.

But I refuse to live as if my depression or Evil will win. I refuse to believe I don't deserve to live.

Sarah has learned that she needs natural buffers for her perceptive abilities. When she was home too much or working in environments that were dense with suffering people, she would get depressed or overwhelmed. She now works in a job with a positive social environment and fewer bits of darkness for her to sense. She can be energized by caring for people and choose how deep to go with them, free of expectations. This has brought out the best in her, and she is doing better now than at any stage in her life prior.

FRIENDS WITH EVIL—ANALYSIS

SUMMARY

A young woman who struggles with self-hate slowly reveals that she has been in a relationship with a dark entity since childhood. This entity convinces her to embrace powerful lies that end up twisting her efforts to love into a deep desire to die.

THE TRAP

"My desire for justice and doing good are powerful. In order to bring good or justice to my friends and family, I will bear pain for them. As time goes on, my desire to harm to myself becomes as strong as my desire to do good."

THE WAY OUT

Four Eyes First

- Respectfully uniting what the helper and sufferer see—this gives access to liberating material (perspective building).

- Sharing insights is a higher priority than a diagnosis or "answer."

Feet Build Trust

- Walk together before trying to change someone's path.

- Everyone has momentum—understand it and move with it.

★

A new interviewer enters with a tray of drinks and snacks. He is a tall, slim man in his thirties with light brown hair and expressive gestures. "Hi, Eric. I can't talk much right now because we have a tight schedule, but I am a former pastor of a large church and was asked by Psyche to talk to you about the story of being friends with Evil. The woman who was here for your first story will be here too, if that's okay. Are you ready to begin?"

He has not told me his name. Again, it feels a little strange, but I want the feedback and reviews for the book, so I just nod. There is something refreshing about the minimal small talk and comfortable silences. Soon after he seats himself, my first interviewer, Ebony, enters, smiles, and slides my summary page to the middle of the table; they begin asking questions. I name the new guy Cross and smile to myself. If they won't tell me their names, they'll have to live with what I name them.

(**Cross**) There are people I know who struggle to know what is psychological, physical, or spiritual when they are hit by hard things. Is it important to figure out which category Sarah was dealing with?

(**Eric**) This is a tough question, because our explanation guides our approach. If I select a label too quickly, I block my ability to see clearly, and my client's ability too. I prefer to leave questions like that unanswered if I don't yet see what the person I am meeting with sees. The work to make *Four Eyes* happen involves the illusive effort of finding what I don't yet know to seek. How is this done?

One of the simplest ways for me to start is by acknowledging that I will never know her or her family as well as she does—to recognize that I bring an outside perspective and she brings an inside perspective. She may misinterpret or give too much significance to an experience, but she holds the inner pool of stories that I need. Some of my favorite counselors spend a large amount of time trying to see the details and structure of their client's unique view of the universe before beginning anything else.

When I share my outside perspectives, I have to make sure they match with the experience, language, and understandings of the person. Many people pretend to have shared understanding, or give the impression of shared experiences, when in reality they don't actually share much. These small dissonances (communicated verbally or nonverbally) are often the most important initial discoveries. They can seem positive or negative, but either can show an area that needs work and care. Sometimes this means preliminary efforts must occur or significant misunderstanding will derail anything that follows.

When our perspectives are shared in mutually beneficial ways, we correct each other, we clarify, and we create new, potent ways of seeing. This is because we have already begun to look outside what we know into uncharted territory—we are learning and growing. Sarah was so committed to her inside perspective that she regularly reinforced the bars of her own jail because she thought she had no other option. She could not pull back to see what she was caught in and needed my broader perspective to reveal more options. The opposite is also true—I needed her inside perspective to understand her jail and then further develop what I could see from the outside.

Work like this should be done to determine if the type of support being given is actually what is needed.

(*Cross*) Why do you think her faith didn't help her more?

(*Eric*) Many traditions teach something like "denial of self," "laying down one's life," "submission," or "detachment." When these are confused or misapplied, they can result in self-harm, even though that's not the intention of the teaching.

We must feed ourselves so that we can give food. We must have a self before we can lay it down. We cannot give away our vitality simply because it is requested or "needed." We must choose where it will give more life: sometimes sacrificing ourselves for another actually makes both parties worse. Within the second greatest Christian commandment lies both sides—"to love our neighbor as *our self*." This is different than loving others at the expense of our self, or our self at the expense of others. Often, wise living gives more to others than a "noble" emotional starvation or death.

(*Cross*) As I hear you talk, I really do agree. If our self is seen as a valuable gift we have been given, we are less likely to fall into such traps. As a gift, it's harder to be prideful because we've done nothing to receive it. Many faiths teach that our body is a temple, a place of reverence, and that we are made in the image of God. Our life ripples outward into many other lives, and in this context, by giving we also receive. As a pastor, I had often fallen into the belief that I had to be a "white knight" who rescued people, but I couldn't see that I was getting stuck in the rescuing role and they were getting stuck as the victim.

(*Eric*) That's why I have been increasingly drawn to this practice of reciprocal dignity. I have also been a one-sided rescuer who took away the chance for people to rescue themselves. I have seen many well-meaning people and organizations accidentally cause harm by confirming destructive, non-reciprocal roles. The humility required to say *I am more than a victim or more than a rescuer can be very hard to learn.*

Epigenetic studies show that harm to one person can carry a destructive legacy forward to many generations, and trauma research shows that harm to one person can bring trauma to those around them. However, we are also all nourished by mutually beneficial relationships, and when that happens we bring a legacy of health and learning.

Reciprocal dignity can include, but goes way beyond, diagnosis and psychological theory. Breaking a human down into their component parts and identifying all the ways they can go wrong can help the healing process, but we must hold such knowledge loosely. We must also see and weigh the whole person and that which surrounds them.

I love to learn about people, and I often enjoy "case studies" that show me how something worked or didn't. Categorizing our understanding about struggles that people have, such as depression, can be helpful simply to identify patterns. However, such categorizations must have less identifying power than the person themselves. This is critical in practicing the *Four Eyes* principle.

I must begin each relationship as if I am a child. I have a great deal to learn (and perhaps unlearn) in order to see through the eyes of the people I am with and to understand how their experiences have shaped and affected them. Each person with schizophrenia has less of their identity tied up in being schizophrenic than not. Each person with bipolar disorder has less of their identity tied up in this label than not. To me, this puts into perspective our categorizations, theories, and therapies.

Something Jean Vanier said has stuck with me: "Wisdom is something that comes, little by little, through a lot of listening." This kind of patient, humble, long-term listening is rare and vitally needed.

(*Ebony*) But Eric, you are departing too far from science. All this mystical talk is nice for making people feel tingly, but ultimately they are missing out on what only science can give. If you step outside objective ways of getting data about people, you are going to be biased. Even if you do good work, you won't be able to share it in ways that are transferable.

(*Eric*) I appreciate those points. I have friends and family members who have dedicated their lives to the empirical, and they hold healthy doubt toward anything that doesn't seem rational or provable. However, the belief that a human can be primarily objective or detached in the presence of another human seems impossible to me. It's like saying you can place two suns next to each other and then pretend there is only one source of light and heat. If this is even partially true, we need other frames of reference to complement the scientific method—the philosophy behind the science we are using, the motivations which fuel a potential application of science, and frameworks for thinking about the unmeasurable and unobservable.

A gentleman I know who carries both mental burdens and brilliance asked me an insightful question related to this issue: "What have you done to cultivate your presence?" The way he asked it prompted a mental image of each person's unique, dynamic identity—their fingerprint—being formed by all their choices and experiences.

This one image has greatly helped my counseling. It inspires me to look for something central when all that seems to be evident are problems and issues. Quakers refer to something like this when they seek "that of God in another." Is it real in the sense that there is a presence within each of us that can be observed directly or indirectly? This is not an easy question to answer. I allow that question to remain unanswered, and it gives me the freedom to continually receive new data and understanding about it.

This concept or image gets closer to the heart of good counseling, because it is often in the intentional overlap of our presences that healing can occur. One colleague calls it "gravity" when a counselor has obtained a weightiness from their beliefs, experiences, and perspectives, so that by being who they are, they help others. It can cause another person to be thirsty for that which is just outside their current understanding. New ideas, hopes, and understandings are naturally created in the space where perspectives join, which could not be credited to any one participant. We can only be thankful that our contribution is not the life-giving whole.

(*Cross*) Is that what you mean by *Feet Build Trust*? I imagined walking together, but you mean also really being together?

(*Eric*) Yes, exactly. Counseling is usually done in an office for the sake of privacy, consistency, and convenience. This is great for some. For others, this is the worst setting. Coming together for the first time is really an invitation into something new.

Walking together can't only mean the figurative sense of having a common experience. Really being together will lead to enjoying each other, laughing together, hearing each other, and feeling known and understood. Sometimes people get scared when they realize I understand more about them than they intended me to. The Feet may need to walk away to recover or reflect before being able to return and walk together. When we honor what a person needs in order to cross a new threshold, we give them the time, space, and security they need to take the risk.

(*Cross*) Can you give some examples about how this played out with Sarah?

(*Eric*) It took quite a while to understand the nature of Sarah's trap. She had almost a lifelong relationship with Evil, like a dear friend when she was little, like a lover when she was an adolescent, and like a master when she was an adult. Talk about power! She had to experience a comparable power to feel enough security to betray her secret. When we shared depth and friendship, she had something to compare to her relationship with Evil.

In having my thoughts alongside her thoughts she made some discoveries:

Not all of the "thoughts" in my head are mine.

- *Example:* If an image of my own horrific death comes
  into my mind and I am repulsed by it, maybe I didn't
  make it.

When she consistently saw how my desires for her freedom stood
up against the comforts of her cage, she learned this:

My desires have been trained in a direction that can lead to inner war.

- *Example 1:* I did not want to be jealous of my brother
  or angry at my parents, so I turned those emotions onto
  myself. My desire to die was a way to keep justice and
  love for my family.

- *Example 2:* When I breastfed as a mother, it was like
  torture because my body was telling me to relax and be
  nurturing, but in the past when I relaxed, I let in dark,
  self-destructive thoughts. Dark thoughts soothed me for
  so long, but they did not fit with motherhood.

When she could tell that I honored her struggle, she was able to
redefine success and reduce guilt when she failed:

Sometimes victory is in living and persevering.

- *Example 1:* I have been tempted to do terrible things
  for so long, but I haven't done most of them—only limited self-harm. This is a victory. I have looked into the face
  of great darkness, confusion, and self-loathing, yet I continue to live.

- *Example 2:* I am very loyal to the kids I work with.

Others would not understand them, and they need me to
know all their little self-care details. For this reason, I stay
in jobs that are very hard for me.

Sarah realized she needed some new "authority" over her who
truly cared about her, so she started calling me her "spiritual dad." She
also began to be with friends and groups that could strengthen her. I
could have pressed her to jump straight into freedom, but that would
have been too much of a change and would not have fit her. Because
I walked with her long enough, I knew this with confidence.

(*Ebony*) There has to be a limit to the idea that the people you are
with are your teachers. Aren't there people who are so wrapped up in
bad things or bad ways of being that you can't get anything but bad
things from them?

(*Eric*) I want to move on to the next story to tackle that question. The
story about Eden is an example of a woman who has given me a great
deal while believing she had little to give. There are people who won't
be able to get past the "bad" things she's done. Early in life, she was
given a vision of herself painted in ugly colors. But she rediscovered
herself in ways that many people do not accept. Her enduringly lovely
heart should have been broken and frozen, but Eden continues to show
me the power that a small core of innocence can have, even inside an
adult whose experiences should have torn it apart.

The interviewers let me end the discussion. Little things like that give me
clues to figure out what is going on. They stand to leave and gather up the
used dishes and containers. I glance down at the table, and the paper with the
piercing eye looks back at me.

I reflect on what allowed Sarah and me to have a good relationship. Somehow, she had to be seen differently than she saw herself. She also needed help to see herself differently, because her false image was so strongly developed. How could this seeing be done consistently? Was this the meaning of the eye I had been given?

As the interviewers exit, I notice an image on the back of Cross's arm. It is a Celtic triquetra, striking because of its fine detail, its vibrant greens and gold. He moves slowly as I take it in; before walking out the door, he turns and looks at me, flexes his arm so I can see it clearly, and flashes me a smile. I sketch the tattoo so I can remember it clearly later.

The image burns into me, entrancing me. The first sketch joins with this symbol in my mind: I imagine each golden section as an eye. Three eyes, three ways of seeing.

*With Kim, **perception** had been needed—looking deeper into the clues she had given to see what was really going on.*

*With Sarah, **perspective** had been needed—linking the small world in which she had been trapped with her place in the larger cosmos seemed to have brought her some freedom.*

Was there a third way of seeing that would allow this symbol to represent what I was encountering? Perspective and perception and . . .

Why was I drawn to this triquetra?

A quiet breeze blows over me. I turn, but see no opening that would have brought it from outdoors.

Dear Reader,

Can an action that appears immoral or harmful help a person grow? If so, does morality have any benefit? It can be challenging to imagine that people are reaching for something worthy while getting something "bad." When women allow themselves to be exploited, or receive physical or emotional harm, they are receiving something from it. This does not mean they made it happen or want it to happen, but if they acquiesce to it or somehow keep it going, their contribution and reason for doing so must be known.

In order to give dignity to the good behind the bad, or to find this "something," it is important to understand the motivation behind the actions. If we can suspend judgement long enough to get more of the real story, the choices and actions start to make sense. However, this will test how far we can carry the practice of reciprocal dignity.

The question I struggle with in the next story is this: Can I temporarily endorse something I don't believe is right or good in order to help the person I am with reach for something better? Not easy.

The form of the story will now change as Eden and I tell it together.

E

I know the world is bruised and bleeding, and though it is important not to ignore its pain, it is also critical to refuse to succumb to its malevolence. Like failure, chaos contains information that can lead to knowledge—even wisdom. Like art.
—*Toni Morrison*

The darker the night, the brighter the stars,
The deeper the grief, the closer is God!
—*Fyodor Dostoevsky*

IV

OF EDEN

A Dream of Wise Counsel
 I walk among them.
 The words we share cause wax to flow unseen from ear to pool;
 A bit of awareness comes holding fear's hand,
 "All is being undone! You are not safe! You are not in control! Run!"

*(**Eric**) My workspace in Eden's school had one wall made almost entirely of glass. It was great because I wanted some protection if I was to meet with a female student alone—the visibility helped with that, but the only way to achieve privacy was to turn your back to the window. Not the easiest place for people who wanted to hide to learn to trust!*

When one of Eden's friends told me she was worried about her, I offered to introduce myself. Eden came to see me soon after, and I was immediately struck by her uncommon qualities: vivid green eyes that were full of depth, tenderness, and loss; gentle, fluid speech. In the movements of her hands there was an uncomfortable shifting and reaching out, a sign of suffering, but not hardness. A piece of her seemed to be frozen in childhood but still alive—it was beautiful and frightening to experience. She was so vulnerable, but she gave off conflicting signals: accessible but guarded, untainted but experienced, somehow unaffected but also wounded. She was stuck open.

As we spoke, it became clear that she did not know how to do normal day-to-day interactions without a sense of awkwardness and fear. Eden hid from me but also drank up our time together, thirsty for something I couldn't name. She rapidly sensed things about me, asked revealing questions about who I was, and examined small details of our conversations like an artist might look at a complex image. Even her vocabulary was a mix of young and old, intentional and unintentional, traditional and secretly different.

(**Eden**) When I reconnected with Eric as an adult, I wondered whether, after nearly ten years, someone who had been so influential in my high school years would affect me in the same way. I tried to recall specific memories of conversations we had had in the past, but only the outlines and feelings stayed with me. I can hardly relate now to who I was then.

In high school I was quiet and labeled as shy. Although I wanted connection, I was fearful of attention that could lead to harm, so I did not take the risk of revealing myself to others.

When you first brought the idea to me of writing my story with you, Eric, I remember you read to me some things you had written about how you remembered me and what you had found uncommon. You described my essence as tender, with a capacity for openness despite my experiences and exceptional suffering. Although my flaws were apparent, you held me in such high regard. I sensed this at the time, but I could not really accept it. I had never been so listened to before, particularly by a man, and it caught me off guard. I sensed life experience and wisdom in you, and it was comforting for me to know that they existed. I needed security to develop into the person that I was becoming, with all of my suffering, questioning, and not fitting into the world. I had no idea how to project that into the future. Because you seemed similarly complex and were someone I could relate to, I could glimpse a world in which fear of non-acceptance didn't need to hold me back. It seemed to me that you had known and experienced suffering and non-acceptance too, and yet you had become an adult who could navigate social situations that required a degree of fearlessness.

As an outsider, you immersed yourself in a school and went about befriending and showing compassion to even the most troubled students. To this day, I consider high schools to be fairly intimidating places; I'm not sure I would dare step foot in one again. They are full of young people who are struggling to find their identities—some by acting out and bullying others, others by hiding or guarding themselves or trying to maintain the facade of popularity. I can't imagine being brave enough to navigate the unpredictability of social interactions with students.

I saw that you remained grounded despite the unpredictability and even hostility that could arise in dealing with bullies or fake people. Everyone seemed to be on the same level with you, deserving of respect and acknowledgement. It's not enough, though, to say you were simply nice or fair to everyone. You somehow drew out the specialness even in students like myself who thought they were unrecognizable.

To be recognized in this way seemed too good to be true or lasting. In the times I met with you, I felt capable of opening up and revealing who I was, but in the days after I always felt doubt creeping in. I wondered if you would lose interest or hope in me, as some of my closest friends had in the past. I feared you would stop reaching out if you didn't see some sign of improvement, if I didn't seem happier or able to open up more fully. You saw so much potential in me, and I was afraid of disappointing you. I kept a lot private and didn't give you many details about the negative things in my life.

Every meeting was a dance. She drew close, noticed her closeness, and withdrew. She offered parts of herself, saw them outside of herself, became nervous and pulled back. I discovered that if I turned down my own intensity by not looking at her as much or by speaking with extra gentleness, she seemed to feel some relief. It was strange to feel connection while still being such a source of anxiety.

There were short windows of time when our dance was forgotten and Eden was full of life and energy. But when she withdrew, it was like the energy of the room was turned down. I imagined this would be exhausting to her and confusing to adults and her peers.

Sometimes Eden would avoid me for a while, but when she did accept an invitation to talk she'd reveal something new. I learned to be patient and accept whatever she would give.

Most of the time, I didn't know where I stood with people (I didn't know what their intentions were or if I could trust them). I needed to know they struggled with life or I couldn't imagine that they were capable of accepting me and my struggles.

Your recognition of my worth was intimidating. It made the stakes high. If I valued the relationship more, then losing it would be harder.

I realized early in my teen years that I exuded a sexual energy that made me noticeable to men. I didn't know if others noticed; perhaps they did and formed an impression about me that was false. It happened with guys my age, but mostly with guys who were older. They looked at me in a way that made me feel desired. I couldn't reconcile that with you, though, Eric. You saw me and maybe recognized that energy, but it didn't seem to intimidate you. It didn't take long before I realized that with you the energy was changed into a different kind of connection, one that wasn't fleeting or sexual.

Throughout high school, I didn't have typical dating relationships—some authentic crushes, but I never pursued the guys I liked. I would sometimes find myself hanging out with guys whose only interest in me was sexual, but I could escape from them before anything happened.

During my senior year, I moved out to live in a rented room in a town near my high school. I no longer wanted to return home, which had become a place of constant fighting and mistrust. As much as I still loved my mom, her relationship with her boyfriend was like a black hole, and I desperately needed to get away from it all. Living on my own, I felt a great emptiness but tried to enjoy my new independence. I went to a few parties, mostly as an observer. My friend Kara accompanied me to places where people were cool, but the experiences only disappointed me and confirmed that I was out of place. I would often end up wandering through town alone, even at night. I usually felt invisible, but there was something peaceful and more authentic in loneliness.

Throughout this time, I met with you, Eric, and didn't tell you the details of what was happening. I knew I wasn't putting myself in the best situations and I didn't want to disappoint you, but you continued to find me and draw me out, and you could always make me laugh.

One day you asked what I thought about you visiting my home and meeting my mother. It seemed to come out of nowhere. In the back of my mind, I thought maybe you had received some information, or that you suspected something concerning or a situation with her boyfriend that you had to look into.

By that time, I felt stuck. Eden and I had a connection, and we were talking about important things, but something was holding her back. Whenever she spoke of her home, I felt a dark, heavy shame. I didn't know why, but I felt that unless we faced her home together, her healing would not happen. In my mind, some insidious harm had been done to her there that she didn't fully

*see. I wondered if it was abuse from a loved one, likely a man, but although
that made sense to me, I didn't quite believe it. It was possibly outside of my
job scope, but I felt strongly that I had to go to her home.*

There was no way I could say yes to what you proposed, but I wasn't
sure how I could avoid it either. I didn't understand your motivation. My mom had always taught me to keep my guard up so no one
would find out bad things, but maybe you got through somehow. At
the same time, I trusted you and I wanted to see some kind of benefit; I hoped that it might help repair my relationship with my mom.

So I agreed to the visit, and when the day came, I felt uneasy and
wanted to keep the conversation superficial. I was afraid you might
ask revealing questions that my mom might misinterpret and get upset with me for later. But you just honored me a little to her. Since
we never had guests at the house, I thought my mom might make a
big deal out of it, but she didn't.

I had been trying to hide my home, to keep that life separate, but
you saw it and still remained in my life. You still thought highly of
me and were able to see my upbringing in an unbiased way. Though
I know you were concerned about the difficult things and their impact on me, you didn't judge my mom or make her into an enemy
or someone you needed to protect me from. The experience was
unique and important to me, and it made me a little more open to
the possibility of not hiding myself to the extent that I had always felt
I needed to.

Eden had a way of passing her emotions to me without words. Even though she'd stay quiet, I could still sense what was happening inside her. The short visit to her home was filled with this dynamic. Somehow this place was an expression of early wonder and the vastness inside Eden; at the same time, it was a place of confusion and loss. Eden's mother gave me the sense that she was a survivor, that she was starved for love and didn't know how to get it. She seemed to take pride in her work and home, but she also gave me the impression that she did not know how to love and appreciate Eden. Seeing them together left me with the sense that they were both doing the best they could with far too little.

After Eden graduated from high school, we connected off and on during her college years, but in her late twenties she was nearing a major set of changes that I knew nothing about when I asked her if she would tell her story for this book. It soon became clear that this was not just a retelling of what I already knew.

In deciding to tell her story, Eden had to take risks. Would bringing up the past bring her back down into it? She had developed new ways of seeing her past that had protected her . . . why mess that up?

When I think of my story, I think of my mother. I don't know much about her young adulthood. She and my dad met in the Southwest and moved north together, even though they were young and had only gotten to know each other through some long road trips. When she was twenty-one years old and pregnant with my brother, they moved to a small rural town, bought a piece of undeveloped land, and put a mobile home on it. My dad left when I was two or three years old, before I had any concrete memories of him.

I was close to my mom when I was young; she said I was attached to her hip. I remember feeling no boundary or separateness between us, and I always wanted to be carried or held. My mom usually worked nights as a waitress or bartender, and sometimes did odd jobs that men typically did, like construction clean-up. When she was home, she worked around the property, so my brother and I played autonomously. We would wander and explore; there was plenty of time for imagination. I would spend the day wading through the creek or laying on the rocks. We didn't have toys or other kids, just freedom and safety to roam.

I remember my mom being sad and staying in bed some days, but it didn't bother me too much. I didn't take it personally. It just felt heavy, and I knew I needed to be away from her. I spent a lot of time observing—I stared at patterns on the couch, particles float-ing through the light coming in through the window, or objects around the room and was captivated for hours. Sometimes I would just lie next to my mom and listen to the sound of her breathing or the sound of rain on the roof, or I'd watch droplets of rain on the window.

For a couple of years after my dad left, she was single, which made that time relatively free of worry and freed more of her attention for us. After that, my mom's boyfriends marked the stages of my life. There were a few boyfriends who were irresponsible and fun-loving, but they didn't stay around for long. I didn't become particularly at-tached to any of them.

I remember there was one boyfriend, though, who was harsh and

would belittle me. I was around six years old. That's when I started being self-conscious and tried to figure out how to avoid his
judgment.

The next boyfriend was generally mean and wanted very little to
do with us. Although it wasn't directed at me or my brother as much,
he pulled more of my mother's attention away from us. She was
caught in the pull of the passion, anger, and conflict. I felt her absence
in those types of relationships.

I really liked the next boyfriend. His name was Dave. I think my
mom was with him from the time I was in second grade until I was
in fifth grade. He was a house painter, had been a hairdresser, and
was different from most men. He was always joking and could make
me laugh uncontrollably. He encouraged me to draw and seemed
to enjoy taking care of us and gave us a lot of attention. I remember
thinking that I must love him as much as my mom. I hugged and
kissed them both before bed. But I also realized how precarious an
attachment it was, knowing that none of my mom's relationships had
ever lasted.

My mom didn't think Dave had a good work ethic and considered
him lazy. He was an alcoholic and would fall asleep on the couch
at night, but he was never mean or harsh. When my mom worked
nights at the bar in town, Dave's dad would watch us until Dave got
off work and could pick us up. His dad made me uncomfortable
when I was left alone with him, coming up with "games" he and I
could play that involved touching him. I wanted him to leave me
alone, and I knew he was being secretive about what he was doing
to me, but it didn't occur to me that I could tell anyone or say no to
him. Dave's dad was doing my mom a favor by watching us, and I

didn't want to make things harder. My brother and I had been in unsafe conditions with babysitters in the past, but it seemed normal to
me that when we were at someone else's house, whatever happened
in that place would stay there. How could Mom know what was happening and do anything about it? She left us there because she needed to and didn't have other options.

One night, Dave came over to pick us up from his dad's house
and saw me on his dad's lap while his dad was having me touch his
crotch. Dave immediately drove us home without saying anything
except to tell me not to fall asleep. I remember looking up at him
while he was driving—his eyes were wide, staring straight ahead at
the road. I could tell he was very angry. I had never seen him like
that. When we got home, he sat me down and patiently asked me
questions, demanding answers. His eyes were full of tears. After that, it
was clear his entire world had been shattered. He would hardly look
at me, and I never saw him happy again.

He and my mom broke up shortly after, and he left. I remember
wishing that no one had found out what had been happening, because it brought so much sadness to Dave, and it meant he had to
leave. Even today, it hurts to think of how much I loved him.

Not long after Dave left, my mom got together with Wayne. Her
relationship with him was the longest, and also by far the worst, relationship she stayed in. For many years, I held a lot of resentment
toward my mom for allowing him into our lives. It was a consuming
relationship for my mom, and it took many years after they finally
broke up before we could start to repair our relationship.

When they got together, I had just started middle school. Until then, not many people in the small town I grew up in had cared about education, and my mom generally distrusted public institutions, so I didn't go to elementary school consistently until around the third or fourth grade. Nearly all of the students were from poor families, so I hadn't felt out of place there—poor school attendance was common, and issues of poverty and substance abuse among families were practically universal.

But middle school was very different. For one thing, I had a forty-five-minute bus ride. The distance allowed for a certain separation; it made my home life something I could keep away from my peers. I also began to notice, from the fancier clothes and different kinds of social interactions, that there was a lot more variation in social status and socioeconomic levels. Kids from well-off families wore brand-name clothing and used their material possessions and appearances to achieve popularity. Other parents picked their kids up from school, concerned themselves with their children's grades and friends, and generally seemed involved in their lives. I generally stayed quiet, preferring to observe in the background.

At home, things with Wayne became unpleasant. He and my mom had violent arguments, and it seemed like my mom was always angry, stressed, or critical toward my brother and me. I started to keep to myself and tried to stay out of the way of either of them. To stay on my mom's good side, I kept up with chores around the house and on the farm, which took up most of my free time outside of school.

Around eighth grade, things got even worse at home. Wayne kept getting fired from jobs for stealing and substance abuse. Many years later, I found out that he had been addicted to meth, but I was oblivious to this at the time.

He also lied to my mother, cheated on her, and had a gambling problem. Though he worked hard, mom had to manage his money. He even stole money from us and used it to gamble. He had a manipulative way of convincing my mother that his addictions were under control, or that he cared enough about her that he would be able to stop doing those things.

Wayne had two kids of his own whom he would see only rarely, but his son came over occasionally. I felt self-conscious around him, and he would join his dad in commenting about my body, calling me names, or pointing out that they didn't need to watch what they ate because they were both very thin. They kept junk food around the house for themselves and would eat it in front of me.

I had a small frame, was of a healthy weight, and had a naturally muscular build, but I came to believe that I needed to lose weight and worried that I would get fatter. My mom would advise me to simply "not eat for a few days." At the time, she was really skinny— now I know that she had an eating disorder. Though she cooked for us, I don't remember my mom ever eating more than a couple bites, which at the time just seemed normal. I thought that I too would have to eat practically nothing in order to stay thin, in part because of our genes (my mom's belief), but also because I was a woman, so of course it mattered that my body look a certain way. I felt more and more ashamed of my body and wouldn't eat for a couple days, and then I'd stay up binging at night. My brother would overeat and was slightly overweight as a teenager, and my mom would hassle him about eating seconds, but there wasn't the same expectation that he should diet or that his life would be ruined if he were somewhat overweight.

Wayne was deceitful and hypocritical, yet somehow my mom continued to fall for his lies. During the times that she would find him out, or when they fought, she would try to reconcile with my brother and me and apologize for being with him. Of course, Wayne was threatened by this, and once my mom was back to believing him, he would find opportunities to take more control and divide us. I never understood why she allowed him to have more authority over us than any of her other boyfriends had.

Seeing how so much of her early life was filled with undependable sources of love and stability helped me understand why relationships were so hard for Eden. She seemed unable to accept things that seemed too good. Even her relationship with me felt at times like she had to talk herself into accepting I was not going to leave, judge her, or stop caring about her. I wanted so much more for her, but had to understand more of her story to see what still held her back.

The summer after I graduated, I had some initial negative sexual experiences with older people. They took advantage of me for being young and not having boundaries. I was seeking closeness and connection, but they were only using me. I recognized how unfulfilling and defeating those kinds of relationships were, and for a time I resolved not to put myself in similar situations, though I continued to feel the pull of intimacy.

College was at first very healing for me because it was a fresh start.

I ended up at a university an hour away from home because I didn't have much guidance on how to apply for college or how to manage the financial aid system.

I became friends with two other students who lived in the dorms. They were young and silly, and it was healing for me to be around them and to focus most of my energy on doing well in my classes. They were both Christian, so I started spending some time in their social circles and went to some of the Christian youth groups they were involved in. The people were welcoming, but I didn't feel that I belonged there.

I had been living off-campus, renting rooms in some difficult situations, but eventually my friends connected me to some guys from their church who were looking for a roommate. We moved into a three-bedroom apartment together in the family housing area of the university.

While there, I met a pretty unconventional guy—he came from an impoverished background like me and was an outcast in his large family, due in part to having been arrested when he was eighteen for having sex with a minor. It seemed like he had been pushed out of society without a chance to redeem himself. He wasn't capable of basic things like paying rent or maintaining a driver's license, but he could survive. He had an inexplicable confidence, and I liked how he seemed free of social pressures. He had resigned himself to a carefree, but meaningless life. He was at the bottom, but seemed free there.

Not long after I had known him, I went to the store with him, and while I waited outside, he was arrested by the police for a past crime. Despite not really knowing him, I felt sad and afraid for him as I watched the police handcuff him. I sent him letters while he was in jail and he started opening up to me. It seemed that kindness had rarely been shown to him in his life, and he had not met someone like me. I could be less guarded with him because I knew he wasn't going to judge me for where I came from. When he got out, I started seeing him and became pregnant. I had to distance myself from my roommates because I sensed their judgement.

I was so nauseous from the pregnancy, I remember there were days I could only lay in a dark laundry room. After several instances of being sick and leaving work, I lost my restaurant job. I felt very depressed and alone. I prayed but did not have any sense that God was with me.

When my mom found out, she insisted that she should raise the baby and would not listen when I said I planned to have an abortion. When I went through with it, she reacted out of spite and said she no longer considered me her daughter. I didn't hear from her after that. I realized that the guy I had been seeing was using me, and that I needed to get my life back by getting away from him and starting over.

I moved to a new college town and into a cramped five-bedroom apartment above a restaurant downtown with my old friend Claire and a few other girls I hadn't known. It was a terrible apartment with green carpet and low ceilings, but I became lifelong friends with two of the other girls, Jess and Sarah, and consider those years to be the best of my life. Our friendships grew at a slow, healthy pace, and there were many nights we stayed up all night talking. They were smart, engaging, and complex. I felt so lucky to have authentic friends who really accepted and understood me. I didn't have to hide who I was with them.

Not long after I turned twenty-one, we went out to an '80s Night at a popular bar downtown. It was crowded and everyone was dancing, but I was observing from a corner of the bar. I caught the attention of a guy named Dane who was a friend of a friend. He was outspoken and told entertaining stories. I thought it was strange that he wanted anything to do with me. Extroverts usually blew over me because I didn't give them enough validation.

After that night, I went out with him quite a bit and found myself caring about him a lot. I spent most of the time with him at his house. I didn't put pressure on him to act like we were in a serious relationship, but it became that after a while. He could draw me out, something I didn't think anyone could do. I was afraid to be seen and would withdraw, but he'd call me out, "Why are you looking down? Look at me." He craved intimacy and had a lot of need to connect, so in a way he forced me to come out of my shell.

We moved together into a garage apartment, and then everything went downhill. Mistrust crept in, and I felt isolated from my other friendships. After drinking, he would often try to provoke me into a fight to make himself feel powerful. If a friend or someone else noticed me, it would set him off. He didn't like my cat or my rabbit. I didn't recognize him when he got mad. As the violence escalated, I had to lie to him about anything that would provoke his insecurities.

One night he came home from drinking and held me down on the bed, yelling at me. I tried to leave, but he blocked the door and slammed it shut as I tried to open it. I went upstairs and lay on the attic floor, and he passed out downstairs. The next day, he knew he couldn't undo that night.

I moved out and started living with an acquaintance, a girl I had gone to high school with who happened to need a roommate and was just moving into a new place. Dane and I weren't breaking up and I didn't want to leave him, but I knew I needed to regain a life outside him to rebuild trust. I remember him coming over to see me at my new place. I didn't know that it would be the last night I would spend with him. The next day he sent me a long email and said he needed us to break up. I couldn't accept that, but when I went to our old apartment the following week to get some of my stuff, I saw another girl's belongings there, and shortly after I saw pictures online of them together.

After that, my reality became a profound experience of suffering. My relationship with my body became disorienting. It was as if it had become so accustomed to being with him that it couldn't be without him. Even looking at my body reminded me that I was no longer with him. I did destructive things, like dating untrustworthy people online, to try to force my body to no longer associate itself with him. I could not accept that he was suddenly gone from my life. It was as though what I had with him never existed.

I started a job cleaning people's houses naked, and also considered working at a strip club after seeing an ad for one. The thought that Dane would find out was terrifying, but part of me also wanted him to know how broken I was, that there was nothing left of the version of me he had known.

Meanwhile, I took prerequisite classes for nursing school at a community college and lived with another high school acquaintance, Raven. She was eight months pregnant when we moved in together, and she had left her boyfriend who had been cheating on her. She was also quiet, and our friendship developed slowly. At first we just helped each other as roommates, but eventually we became like a family.

I watched her baby while she went to her classes. I didn't have any previous experience caring for children, but wanted to be a helpful, supportive person to her.

When she came home from the hospital after giving birth, I remember she handed her newborn right over to me, smiling confidently, and I sensed an enormous amount of trust from her.

I never felt I had to hide my pain from her, and I don't think that I could have at the time. It was very profound for me to develop a bond with someone despite being in a state of suffering. I would get messages from my ex-boyfriend and feel a wave of panic in my body, but I could still go into her room and watch TV or talk to her as a relief from the heaviness of my thoughts.

Raven introduced me to the writings of Eckhart Tolle by letting me borrow some of the audiobooks she had, like *The Power of Now* and *A New Earth*. Everything he spoke of resonated with me deeply, and even if only for the time I spent listening, my racing, anxious mind slowed down. I felt a peace I had never known before. I started to accept my suffering and see beauty in my everyday life, in the smallest things. I became aware of the patterns of my thoughts and emotions and could watch them, almost in curiosity; I wondered at the momentum that kept them going.

Strangely, at the same time that I felt this peace and even stability, I worked up the nerve to start dancing at a strip club. It was a small dive bar about an hour and a half away.

The first time I went on stage for an audition, I was visibly shaking. I had watched some of the other girls, but I had no idea how to move my body in the same ways. Every person in the bar—the bartenders, the DJ, the other dancers, all of the customers—stared at me. I could sense the emotions, the empathy and judgement directed at me (mostly from the other dancers). Somehow, I survived and managed to undress by the end of the song. Though it didn't feel natural at first, I received so much positive reinforcement that it was easy to get better at it. Within a few months, I felt at ease on stage; I learned how to move and how to do pole tricks. I was amazed that my body could move so gracefully and that it was capable of such strength. I also had to challenge myself to talk to strangers, to initiate conversations, and to capture someone's interest. Prior to dancing, I had very little relatable experience in doing this. I started making good money, and dancing actually felt much safer than some of the other destructive escapes and situations I had been putting myself into.

It was a relief to do something with my sexuality and my body that, in a sense, relieved the loss of intimacy I had suffered after losing Dane. I could show compassion and intimacy to strangers who least expected to find it there, and they seemed grateful for it. I didn't feel as if those interactions were false, even though the context was, of course. I had enough understanding of suffering and what people do with suffering that I didn't judge the men I danced for. It felt natural to listen to them. I felt comfortable sharing their physical space, showing my body to them, and even looking into their eyes in the way that I only ever had with Dane. I knew what it felt like to rest in someone's gaze like that, to be in awe of the depth of a person who can be so close and still seem completely foreign and unknowable. It felt good to make others feel recognized and embraced in that way, despite their reasons for being there, their flaws, their age, or other factor that would create separation in other circumstances.

I felt an openness and fearlessness toward the world. Though I encountered many negative, harsh situations, I felt relatively unaffected by them. Perhaps I felt that nothing compared to the loss that I had experienced. Having risked entering a role weighted with so much stigma from the outside world, I felt somehow incredibly free, as though I had chosen to face judgement and instead found truth in the darkest places.

I moved to a larger city to start nursing school and worked in nicer and bigger clubs. I made a lot more money, but the clubs were far less regulated and the private dance areas weren't as closely monitored. I had to create and enforce my own boundaries, which wasn't easy. Some men were intent on mistreating me, trying to take control, or doing things against my will. There were times I was relatively passive and allowed this kind of treatment, or only tried to divert it indirectly. While those moments could be unbearable, I sometimes had a powerful and strange realization that I was still myself. I was not disassociated from my body, but rather inhabited it completely. When I felt connected to myself in that state, I realized I could not be diminished. It seemed almost paradoxical that I felt stronger as a result. I became increasingly intolerant of being mistreated. Encountering the same situations over and over provided me with opportunities to create boundaries.

Sometimes this meant simply turning men down for dances when I recognized red flags, stating my boundaries before dancing for them, yelling at them to stop doing something, forcibly removing their hand from my body, or getting up and leaving without finishing the dance.

For several years, I felt suspended in the hidden, isolating world of dancing, but I didn't want to escape. On stage and in private dances, I was being seen and regarded in a way I never had been by the outside world. In some way, I felt my essence being reflected back to me through what they saw. I spent countless hours getting ready for work, straightening my hair and putting on makeup. People who knew me previously would have hardly recognized me. Altering my appearance to such an extent allowed me to experience at work what it is like to be considered conventionally beautiful.

Some nights after work, I felt this momentous energy that I didn't know what to do with when I got home, but dancing was also physically and emotionally exhausting. I had saved so much money that I hardly saw the value of it anymore when I would sit on the floor, tediously counting it after my shifts. I wasn't afraid of not getting by anymore, as I had always been in the past. The thought of returning entirely to an unseen life outside of dancing seemed inconceivable, but I knew I couldn't do it forever.

I continued to have a strong relationship with Raven, although we lived far away from each other. She was in a long-term, committed relationship with a man and had another child with him. Our lives had become very different and separate. At times we had little to relate to one another, and this weighed on our friendship. All the while I had been dancing, I didn't date anyone I thought wouldn't accept my dancing, and therefore my relationships were shallow. The few I had were with men I met through work, who knew of and accepted the fact that I danced. I hardly acknowledged that I was in relationships with them. I didn't feel like I needed them or like it would hurt to lose them.

The thought of leaving the dancing world filled me with anxiety and dread, but I was nearing the end of a very rigorous nursing program, and the expectation to start working in that field loomed ahead. Although my grades had remained perfect, I always felt like I was on the brink of failure. I regularly stayed up entire nights studying and was in a state of constant stress and fear. I neglected all my other needs—for sleep, regular meals, and social connection. I started to have migraines and tension in my body that made it difficult to fall asleep. I was afraid I'd be found out, that I didn't belong in the professional world.

After I graduated, I postponed taking my licensing exam for six months and didn't actively apply for jobs for a year. During that time, my attention was not as divided since I was no longer absorbed by the stress of school. The days seemed to blend together. I started to think I had gained everything I needed from dancing, and that I might be ready to move on.

Eventually, I began applying for nursing positions and accepted my first job.

This was Eden's first major step away from dancing. It was like breaking an addiction, and I hoped she would keep going. My family traveled near Eden's current home, so we set up a meeting at a restaurant. We had been talking about her life story on the phone, and at times it had left her shaken and wondering if her suffering had any meaning or good in it. Her mother came for a visit and stirred up old feelings, causing Eden to wonder if the past had been worth experiencing or bringing up again. Wasn't she supposed to live in the present?

As my family ate their meal in another part of the restaurant, Eden and I caught up, laughed, and talked about life. Her laughter and jokes came faster than in the past. We contemplated together how her shyness protected her exquisite perception and her inner life that could not be harmed by all the harshness she had experienced; how her deep pains were evidence of a capacity for deep relationship and deep contemplation of life's many wonders; and we both hoped she would find people who saw her like those of us who really knew her. Tears glistened in her eyes for much of the conversation. Later, after I was home and on a phone call with her, I asked about her tears at the restaurant. She said it was so refreshing to be understood, known, and honored. They had been tears of joy.

After seeing you, it felt as though my soul had come up to the surface. I was so grateful to have had the chance to see you and found it just as easy to sit and talk to you as it had been in the past. You are just as lively and perceptive as ever, although you seem much taller than I remembered and have *slightly* more wisdom in your eyes when you smile.

As Eden caught me up on the years during which we had not communicated, I could see that she had cobbled together a skillset and relational foundation through a combination of harm and good. She still couldn't accept things that were too good because she felt too different from them, but she'd learned to find good in incredibly dark and hostile circumstances. She had grown, despite so many experiences in which she disrespected herself. Dancing was the relationship school she needed, even as it blocked her from being respected and

loved. Her lessons came at a high price—she had faced so many fears to liter-
ally stand naked before the world, and in doing so she had found that part of
herself that could not be diminished. This insight is powerful no matter how it
is found.

Our most recent communication happened over text. I told her: "I want
you to remember that you can't disappoint me. You can't change the high re-
gard that I have for you. I hope you become ready to talk again, and what we
talk about does not have to be only about the hard things. I just want you to
know that I still care."

She wrote back, saying,

Well, the first and biggest thing is that I'm going to be a mom
in about seven months. I'm happy and feel mostly ready. I'm
looking for new jobs because I won't be able to manage the
commute I've been making after my long shifts when I'm
late in my pregnancy. This Saturday will also likely be my last
dance shift, and I haven't really processed that yet. And then
I'm going to visit my mom all next week.

My questions had to wait. Eden withdrew after that. She would give little
acknowledgment to my invitations to talk, and we didn't reconnect for many
months. Finally, just before it was time to give birth, she told me she was
"nesting" and fixing up her home for the baby. She had a new strength and
clear direction that I enjoyed hearing about. I didn't want to disrupt her peace,
but asked enough to discover that she had initially kept knowledge of the
pregnancy from the father; he had been in the United States illegally and had
since gone home. Eden released him from responsibility and prepared to raise

the child on her own. It was one of the few things she could do to break her tie to dancing and create a clear, loving relationship.

I'm waiting to hear about the baby, and in the meantime I pour out the love and respect I have for her and hope she embraces it. I hope she will be receptive to real love when it comes: Eden, please see your heart, mind, and beauty as noble. You no longer need transactional boundaries to be cherished. You have built them yourself and can do it again. You are worthy of being the delight and honor of another.

The waiting is interrupted by a lovely text:

"Hi Eric, we are doing well. We had some rough patches early on and still have a lot of challenges, but overall things are starting to get easier."

My phone was flowing with baby pictures, and Eden and I were reconnected. She explained the need to have a very protected delivery and time to get into a pattern of feeding and care. She also acknowledged that she was concerned some of my natural inquisitiveness might lead to questions she didn't want to think about at the time and some she still wasn't ready to answer. We set up some parameters so it would be easier to hold certain conversations only when the timing was right, and we redefined my role in the new family. I was granted honorary uncle status as well as family jester, but only when summoned.

OF EDEN—ANALYSIS

SUMMARY

A young woman is raised in an environment with the potential to develop a rich, deep inner life, but through many unsafe men, she comes to believe that she must remain hidden. She attempts to climb out by attaching to more broken men, but finds a way to set new rules for herself through exotic dancing and pregnancy.

THE TRAP

"Tainted good is the only good I am comfortable with, and this keeps my attractions and nourishment impoverished. I find dignity in primal ways because they are the best I can get."

THE WAY OUT

A Dark Pond Still Holds Water

- Climbing out of darkness might require standing on shadows.

- Seemingly bad outcomes can contain hidden good.

Good Appetite, Good Human

- Regularly receiving good takes experience and practice.

- Giving more good requires receiving more good.

★

Ebony and Cross enter again after giving me a short break—maybe to talk about what they were analyzing (the stories or me)? They carry a small package wrapped in brown paper and zealously taped up. I find myself excited to continue. Part of me wonders if I am being foolish. I am telling them very private information about myself without any sense of wanting to withhold or limit it. I had agreed to the interview thinking the transcripts might be helpful for the book, but I wonder if they may have me here for more than an article about my writing.

As I reflect on this possibility, I am struck that the idea doesn't bother me. I discover that I like these people despite the disjointed, mysterious nature of the whole process.

They place the Summary, Trap, and Way Out paper on the table and the package next to it, as if they are familiar enough with both items that they aren't needed. The conversation begins.

(**Ebony**) Are you using the term Dark Pond to describe people?

(**Eric**) A false perception of people, focusing on the negative or bad about them.

(**Ebony**) Is the water the good that is in them?

(Eric) Yes, and it also refers to the person who is seeing the water. To practice this principle, the observing person must be able to look past or through the darkness in order to see who the observed person really is. In Eden, the barrier was not external; she is beautiful. However, some early readers of her story were troubled by her exotic dancing and my finding any good in it. Can a person love Eden without understanding why she dances? Would she let someone care about her if that remained a secret? Would it be good for her if someone convinced her that dancing was simply her choice? The answers to these questions become clear (like water) when she is really known.

*(**Cross**)* Are you naturally good at seeing past the bad and into the good, or did you get some training on how to do this?

(Eric) I get it in part from my mom. She is incredible at finding ways into the hearts of people who appear to be socially unacceptable; she is drawn to people others would ignore or dismiss.

Once we were staying at a bed and breakfast in Germany, and the proprietor appeared to despise us and perhaps life in general. His face was frozen in a perpetual lemon-puckered scowl. When we appeared for breakfast a few minutes late, he declared, "Breakfast is no longer served." The rest of us grumbled and marveled at the poor service while my five-foot-two-inch mother sashayed over to the man and spoke kindly and gently to him. She asked questions and beamed at him with her warm smile. Soon they were arm-in-arm and he was giving her a tour of the place, complete with intimate details of his home/business. I saw on his face a slight upturn of mouth. He was remembering old joys through my mother's attention and care. It was giving him a bit of energy, hope, and renewal. Soon we were eating breakfast and all seeing the situation quite differently.

My mother's example has served me well when an apparently closed person comes through the door to meet with me. She didn't set out to teach me this way of being, but by being herself, she's a part of what I do.

My daughter has taught me how to see past "disabilities," especially when, in a moment of insight, she referred to herself as "a little girl trapped in a teenager's body." Her autism affects how she sees the world and herself. She doesn't understand things like swearing: "Why would someone choose to use words that are wrong and hurtful?" It's stressful for her to hear a person do something that is so clearly "bad." She can't let it go. Is this a disability or something else?

Being younger inside than she appears reveals harshness in life that people who develop more typically accept as normal. It's an incredible barrier to have part of one's self held back from social conformity and still have the expectations of the world for your age placed upon you. Society often views childlike adults as broken, but in my experience it is often this sheltered part of a person that allows them to be the most vibrant, creative, loving, and perceiving. If this is understood, a person can learn how to protect and share that tender part. My daughter's example in this continues to teach me as she naturally relates and as she expresses some of her rare perspective through artistic crafting.

(*Cross*) If your children had been easy and typical, you wouldn't have learned that. It seems like it would have been easy to crush what was best about her to make her fit in.

(Eric) Very true. My wife and I joke that without our struggles we likely would have thought we knew a lot more about parenting than we did.

(Cross) What about people who hide or guard their good "water"? Is it hard to know that it's even there?

(Eric) In many of my experiences with suffering women, I have sensed part of them was hidden away like a child in a cage. They often hide for protective purposes initially, but then it can be difficult to know how to get her back out. By the time I see these women, their lives have been consumed by an effort to pretend an important part of themselves isn't missing. In the midst of fear, they somehow internalize the message that they are not enough or are too much.

In these situations, a high degree of trust is needed for the integration of "selves" to occur. It could be said that these are less severe forms of what was clinically called Multiple Personality, or currently, Dissociative Identity Disorder. When a portion of a person that is productive, tough, or detached is forced to the front, it can be rewarded in many settings. However, relationships often reveal that a tenderer, younger, vibrant, creative part is missing. Tough, stressed, or hostile exteriors often shield something worthy of protection and value.

(Ebony) So, is *Good Appetite, Good Human* attempting to help the downtrodden receive more of the good that is already in them?

(Eric) I have to clarify what you mean by downtrodden, because when I began consulting, I was surprised to see how many talented and respected people came to see me. "High-functioning" people

often had breakdowns because they were not extended the grace sometimes offered to obviously struggling people. They were so good at hiding, people didn't realize they were in trouble. Often the help had to come in a way they didn't expect so that their automatic defenses *fueled by their strengths* did not block the effort.

(*Ebony*) So we all need to develop our appetite for receiving good?

(*Eric*) We all have appetites or needs because we all have to receive and relate in order to grow. When we fill up on anything, we become familiar with the process through repetition and sensory pleasure. We have a choice as to what we fill up on. We can become used to filling up on things that don't really meet our need—porn, unhealthy foods, detached or destructive relationships. This leaves us with a false fullness that masks a real void.

When I meet with people who are wounded but have an open, curious heart and mind, and if I am able to have the same, then discovery and creation happen. This builds on what we already are, have, and know. Our early development trains us with patterned, repetitive behaviors, and these things become normal, but "normal" is often a mix of that which helps us grow and that which does not.

Just like foods or smells become connected to feelings and experiences, so do other things we "feed" ourselves with.

(*Cross*) Would *Good Appetite* affect our attractions or interests?

(*Eric*) Yes. When I was a teen, it used to drive me crazy to see lovely, smart girls get attracted to guys that so obviously treated them badly. I wanted them to date me, but I could see that there was something they were drawn to in the bad guys. I ended up informally interviewing many girls and women about why they were attracted to something they knew was bad for them.

One theme kept coming up which surprised me. Kindness and other qualities they really wanted had become uncomfortable and even repugnant to them: "I feel bad because he is so good"; "I don't know why he would need me"; "I'm not enough like him"; "If he really knew me, he wouldn't like me."

When talking about "bad guys," they would say things like, "He needs me"; "I know what to do with a guy like him"; "He seems so in love with me… sometimes." They often described being caught in cycles that they couldn't quite see or get out of. These cycles left them diminished, while the guy got what he wanted. We will get into more of this topic in the next story, but the main idea I learned from the interviews was that these women had to get used to receiving more good—they had to become familiar with the vulnerability of receiving goodness, opening their hearts in new ways, discovering untended parts of themselves, and trusting in trustworthy people.

(*Ebony*) Thank you for talking about this story. I found it personally helpful to know about a woman who could have so many bad things happen to her and still hold so much good inside.

As the interviewers again stand to depart, the package sits on the table untouched. They don't mention anything about it. Having had my fill of this cryptic behavior, I blurt out, "Should I open the package?" They smile and walk out silently. I mutter, "Well then, I guess I get to decide," and lift the tape and paper to reveal an unmarked white box. Beneath the lid, I find crumpled paper balls and another small box.

Inside the second box is a device similar to a cell phone, but when I turn it on, it has only a single app. The app appears to be a generic voice recorder, and when I tap on it, an old woman's voice speaks. Its strength and clarity give me the physical sensation of awe. I have witnessed something rare. She speaks only a single sentence:

"There's no such thing,
as a wise and evil king."

I play the recording over and over, just to hear the voice. So old, so alive, so playful, so powerful. On the seventh playback, the device powers off. I try to turn it back on but get no response. Not even an empty battery symbol. I feel loss.

Thinking about the meaning of the words, I can't recall any story where a king, or any character, really, is both evil and wise. Why is that? Is wisdom inextricably linked to goodness? Does wisdom have to be rooted in a person?

I know Psyche Journal focuses on wisdom in philosophy and psychology, and they said they would interview me about my stories, but this is getting strange. I realize I don't know very much about this organization. I remember the cover of their magazine has a sun on it. It's a warm, generous image which appears to cast light and heat as a gift for the solar system. It seems to show great power used for great good.

I sketch what I remember on the back of one of the pages on the table:

The sun has been seen as a symbol of goodness because its light, heat, and great power are offered to the just and the unjust and to the empty places beyond and between planets, as well as being a center for them to orient around. It is as if wisdom is woven into the fabric of the universe in the form of this expansive goodness, as well as in the good insights which guide the healthy relations of life. I am moved, like I've received a new glimpse of wisdom in these many forms.

As some minutes pass, my mind shifts to my next story, because I can't figure out what the agenda really is for this strange set of meetings. At least the next story brings me back to a familiar young woman. As I think of her, I recall that her physical beauty did not protect her from degradation. Her tattoos, piercings, and constantly boiling shame taught me about a central human need.

Dear Reader,

It is painful to see innocence harmed, beauty soured, or darkness fall over the good. This is not the experience of a few; we are all on this road to varying degrees. The consequences follow familiar patterns—withdrawal, hostility, frozen lethargy or apathy. These are the automatic responses to high stress (fight, flight, freeze) played out into relationships.

Yet there is something in the eyes of a young child, the tender-hearted old dependable servant, or the trusting, receptive animal companion which calls us back to what we were and still are. Thoreau described this when he said, "Through our own recovered innocence we discern the innocence of our neighbors." Picasso did as well: "It takes a very long time to become young." We must learn how to live in a sometimes hostile world. We have choices as to how it is done and what parts of ourselves are given primacy. We may need help to see that we have a choice and what that choice entails if this was never shown to us.

The next story reveals what happens when an exploiter takes advantage of someone who is not able to defend herself. However, looking into the heart of the exploiter, we also see "that which was not given." Hiding behind force and charm leaves a hollowness that can be filled in a better way. As long as justification hides the truth, this will not be accomplished. We also see in the exploited a strength and vibrancy that appeared to have been destroyed, but with an increased appetite for the good, that "sacred child" inside shows her worth—and it is beyond measure.

E

For children are innocent and love justice, while most of us
are wicked and naturally prefer mercy.
—*G.K. Chesterton*

V

DEADLY CHARM

A Dream of Wise Counsel

So much rests on these moments of expansive trust or shriveling safety.
A shaking step, a fountain of tears, exhaustion, mortification,
A death of the built me —
Walls break, systems crumble — what was alive is alive again but so
*   small, so fragile.*
Is this really better than what was? Can I be a slave again?

*(**Eric**) When I first met Akira, she had broken away from her abusive father and husband to live with her aunt and uncle while trying to rebuild a life with her young son. She told me, "Moving here, being around people who love me just for being me, is amazing!" She was also amazed to see herself succeeding in her dental tech studies. But her husband was still lurking around, trying to suck whatever life he could from her. Akira explained:*

(**Akria**) My aunt encouraged me to get work, so I applied for a grant to become a dental hygienist. I cried with excitement when I got it—I paid $350; they paid $3000! I was succeeding! But my husband Frank tried to get me to borrow it all from him.

"Move back in with me and I will pay all your school costs."

"I don't need your money!" I said. He was proud and angry at the same time.

"I don't like you becoming so independent," he said.

Every A I got, he would cut down, like, "If you get a ninety-seven percent, I will buy you a car." It was his way of saying that my A wasn't high enough and to make the rewards come from him, as if he made the grades happen.

Her aunt was aware enough to realize that she and her family could not give Akira all she needed. She knew Akira had to have a place to sort out the massive culture differences between her new home and her abusive homes. She told me, "We need to find what's holding Akira back so that she can keep moving forward." I felt the danger of being a man trying to build trust with her when her experiences had taught her that men were manipulative and unsafe. I needed to understand what made love hard for Akira to receive and what was confusing about her new home. So in our first meeting I asked, "Why is it sometimes hard at your uncle and aunt's house even though you know they love you?"

I don't want to be a burden. I drive my younger cousins around a lot, but I need gas money or I can't do it. They don't know how much food I buy for the family with my food stamps, so it's hard for me to ask for gas money and have them wonder how I am spending it. I take pain relievers for my back and they worry I am abusing them. I don't want them to worry about me.

One time I asked to go home from a family gathering because my son was getting tired. There was resistance. It felt like I was asking too much in taking one of them away from the party to drive us home. I felt like someone who shouldn't be there.

Meanwhile, my husband calls me constantly, trying to get me to come back to him. He sends flowers and chocolates and won't take no for an answer. He pretends he is calling for our son (which is the only reason I accept his calls), but then he tries to flirt or connect with me. When I visit his apartment so he can spend time with our son, he often tries to kiss me or put his arm around me or slap my butt. Sometimes he shows up at my uncle and aunt's house and they have to help me stop him. It's so stressful!

It can be hard to discipline my son and not sound like my dad or husband. I feel like saying, "You know better. You should get beaten if you are disrespectful or disobey me." My aunt tries to show me other ways, but I feel like she doesn't think I am doing a good job as a mother, and it makes me mad. I want to say, "Don't treat me like a kid. I'll work this out."

They give me so much, and my life has been changed because of their love, but I don't want to be a burden. If I feel like a burden, I want to leave.

It wasn't long before Akira graduated with very good grades and got a job with a dentist. Things were looking up, and she announced that she was moving into her own apartment. Her family was worried that it was too soon and that she may not know how to choose a good community for herself. But Akira was determined to live on her own.

I have to prove I can do it. I got child care for my son. I found an apartment and fought for it. "Send the paperwork right now," I said to the property manager. "Run the credit check. If I have to, my aunt will be my 'roommate' to prove it will work!"

I have to prove that the men in my life were wrong about me, that they didn't have a right to control me because I was their daughter or wife. I have to move into my own apartment so I can feel what it's like to be free—to spend my money on coffee and making my nails look pretty—and not be dependent on anyone but myself.

I had forgotten about myself for so long, but that's changed. I have control of my money, and good things are happening because of my hard work.

But it wasn't easy and Akira had many unusual setbacks in the first few months of being on her own. She so badly wanted to be free, but Frank pushed her to depend on him whenever the chance arose.

Bad things seem to follow me. As soon as I get a little money, I have to spend it. People don't see all that I pay for, and they think I am irresponsible when I spend some on fun things. I work very hard and am barely holding it together.

Once, I got into a car crash and had to borrow Frank's car until mine was repaired. It took months. He tried to hold it over my head to get things from me. At the same time, I had three jobs in a row that suddenly ended even though they said I didn't do anything wrong. I had almost zero savings, so those times were very scary and confusing. A neighbor even tried to get me to do sexual things and groped me. It was boring being out of work, so I got caught up in wanting to fight back at Frank. I pretended to be other girls on social media to see what he would do, and he had no problem flirting with these fake girls. I messed with him like he messed with me until I saw it wasn't doing any good.

To help Akira set some limits, her aunt and I set up a meeting with Frank.

Akira was going to confront him on his continued disrespect and we would help her.

When the four of us met together, the thing that made me the angriest was when he implied I should be working harder! I work so hard! He also made it seem like if he just did more for me, then I would come back to him. He wanted to "never give up" on our relationship, but that just sounds like he will never respect my limits. He disrespects me constantly, but I can't stop him, because I feel bad for him and my son needs a father. I would divorce him, but I need the money the army pays me while we are still technically married.

Frank was like a hollow man to me. He knew how to be smooth and get people to like him and do what he wanted, but when you got past his charm and bravado, he was needy and scared. He knew how to use even those feelings to make women connect to him, but he didn't know how to be good to them. He seemed shifty, trying to impress, trying to manipulate . . . a boy trying to be a man. His persistence was strength in some ways, but he seemed to go after the wrong things—often what was not his to take. Akira made it clear over and over again that she wanted to move toward a divorce, but it was hard for her to hold that line. I tried to help find a person he would listen to, but Akira believed he trusted only himself. She wondered if he would listen to me, so I agreed to try.

I talked with Frank separately and let him know that it was over with Akira, and that any pursuit of her would be a violation of her wishes. He acted sad, but seemed to understand that this was true. He gave her some space for a few weeks and then he was at it again. I felt a strange mix of sorrow and compassion, as well as anger at how many ways he would manipulate and harm Akira and other women to make himself feel better.

Akira had some relief in confronting and setting some limits with Frank that day. She seemed to trust her aunt and me more afterward, as if our helping her take control was a language she understood. The next time we met, she was ready to talk about Frank and how she had become so tightly tied to him.

Frank came to the US when he was twelve. He didn't speak any English and kids made fun of him for it. He focused on learning English so that he could fit in. He worked hard and became good at it. Eventually, he found he could make girls interested in him by saying "the right things." He thought he was hot stuff in junior high and high school, but when he joined the military and started wearing a uniform, there was no stopping him.

When I first met Frank, I didn't want to be with him. We met at a club, and when he first asked for my number, I said no. But after we danced together for a while, he put his phone in front of me, and I automatically entered my number. We texted nonstop for a couple of days and he was smooth, said all the right things, and was charming and good at making me smile. We ended up hanging out a lot and were inseparable until he was deployed. Even while he was gone, he still managed to make me feel important and needed, and he was there for me whether I needed help financially or just wanted to talk.

We rarely ever fought . . . until I started getting Facebook messages from his ex-girlfriends. They tried to tear me down, saying things like,

"He would never choose you over me," and threatening me.

When I told Frank about it, he said, "You shouldn't have argued back," or "Just ignore them," or "I'm not getting involved."

I noticed that any time other females were involved, he wouldn't defend me.

Deployments were twelve months long, and all the soldiers got to go home for two weeks at a time. He so badly wanted to go to Florida to see his family that it made me really jealous. Frank ended up buying me a round trip ticket to Florida to stay with him at his mom's house. I hadn't met his family before, and being Haitian, some of them didn't speak much English.

He was late picking me up at the airport, so we started off on the wrong foot. I got the royal treatment at his mom's house, but I could tell that things were off between Frank and me even though I was so excited to have my two weeks with him. His mom loved me and took me to her Haitian friends' houses to show off her son's white girlfriend. She had always wanted one of her sons to be with a white girl so she could have mixed grandkids.

It had been a great few days, but then it all went downhill because of Frank's little four-year-old niece. She didn't like me at all! Any time she saw Frank and me cuddling or holding hands, she would get between us.

One day she came up to see me in the room Frank and I were sharing and said, "Who are you?"

I said, "I'm Akira, Frank's girlfriend."

She said, "No, you're not! Betty is Frank's girlfriend! I saw them kissing!"

I said, "Oh, you did? When did you see them kiss?"

She said, "Today! On this bed!"

I called Frank up into the room and told him what his niece said. He laughed like it was a joke and then called his niece a snitch. "We weren't doing anything; we were just talking, I promise!"

I had told him from the beginning not to play me like a fool because I would always catch him, but he stuck to his story.

A couple of awkward days went by. Since his mom didn't speak English, she and Frank spent a lot of time speaking Creole; but when it was just Frank, his older sister, and me, he would still speak Creole just so I wouldn't know what they were talking about. Frank got a laugh out of keeping me out of the loop and making me look dumb.

I started noticing that this was not the Frank I knew. He had no problem parading me around to his friends, but he wouldn't take me on a date. Everything he did in Florida was with his friends, but he left me out.

I also noticed he was more protective of his phone, iPod, and laptop than before he deployed. One day when I asked to see his phone, he got defensive and told me no, so I knew something was up. I had been cheated on in every relationship I had been in previously and I caught them all because I'm like the FBI. So I found a way to check his devices and found sexual conversations between him and multiple girls from his hometown, even naked pictures. My heart dropped. My world was crushed by a man once again, and I just started bawling!

When I got it together, I asked him about everything and his answer was that deployments were hard and it gets lonely.

"So when you're at work or you can't talk to me," he said. "I get bored, and then I just start talking to other girls. I like to see if I still got game and see what I can get them to do." I was dumbfounded! I couldn't believe what I was hearing.

After he gave me that answer and he saw me crying and hurting, he tried to hug me, but I pushed him away. He just kept saying, "Babe, please, I'm sorry! I never meant to hurt you. Those girls mean nothing to me, but you mean the world to me!" Just those words made me feel important, and his begging for forgiveness made me feel like I had all the power. After using words, he always turned to material things: "Let's go to dinner—let me take you on a shopping spree—we can do whatever you want, just *please forgive me.* It will *never* happen again." There would be puppy eyes, gentle hand kisses, and hugs. He'd hold me tightly and whisper, "I'm sorry, baby! Please forgive me! I don't want to lose you!" Then I'd crack and believe him. For some stupid reason, I always believed him!

He started out a dream come true and made all these promises to me: "I promise I'm not like other guys. I promise to never hurt you or cheat on you. I promise to make you smile. I promise to always be there for you. I promise I will never lie to you or go behind your back." But recently Frank admitted, "When we got together, I wasn't who I truly am. I was putting on an act to try to win you over because you made me fight for it. I like the thrill of the chase. I did what I had to and made you believe what I needed you to believe so that I could win you over." He even had the guys he was working with help him text me romantic things every morning.

As Akira described the details of her life, she discovered patterns she had never seen before. She was amazed by the things that kept sucking her back to Frank and, as it turns out, back to her father. They had both told her she was stupid because they knew they were manipulating her and she kept genuinely caring about them. It made her confused because sometimes they did care about her, or at least "needed" her. As she saw the complete story of her life, she was able to gain a little distance from it, and the manipulations had less power over her.

As we met over the course of months, Akira would say, "I have never felt time go by so fast!" and "I can't believe I talked so much all at once!" and "I feel good about being with you and talking with you . . . it is so different than what I am used to." We kept discovering early skills and experiences that she simply never received. I regularly had to conduct little tests to see what she knew about relationships, power, and herself, because there were hidden gaps:

- *Do you think a two-year-old should be 'beaten' if they disobey knowingly?*

- *What does loyalty to someone you love look like?*

- *Do you deserve to be treated badly?*

- *Can forgiveness be given too quickly or easily?*

One story revealed how hard it was for her to see the difference between one-sidedly taking care of someone and mutual love:

Frank ended up getting shot in the leg and hip and had to be flown back to the States to get medical care. Because we weren't married, the first person the army called was his mom, and she met him in Virginia. He had always been a momma's boy, so he was more than happy to have her there taking care of him. I wanted so badly to go see him. My boyfriend was shot twice by an enemy sniper, but he didn't want to hurt his mom's feelings by telling her that he wanted me to be the one to take care of him. I felt unwanted and not important enough to be there with him. A couple days passed before he had the army fly me to Virginia to help take care of him when his mom had to go back to Florida to work. I arrived at the hospital, and I remember seeing him there in the hospital bed with his leg in a huge sling; he was so skinny!

I walked into the hospital room and his mom, sister, and niece all stared at me—I hadn't realized they'd be there, so that felt weird. But his family left a couple of days later, and we were soon moved out of the hospital into the barracks, which were like mini apartments. We had dated for about a month before deployment, had those two bad weeks in Florida, and now suddenly we were living together so that I could take care of him! I had to push him in his wheelchair up a long sidewalk to all his appointments and all our meals in the middle of winter. I had to help him with at-home physical therapy and he never made it easy. He wanted to pretend like he was doing therapy, but he really wasn't. He wouldn't meet with his social worker, so I had to snitch on him because I wanted to see him get better. I had to change the dressings on his leg, bathe him, mostly clothe him, and grab things that he needed that he couldn't reach because he was relearning how to walk. I was his live-in wife/maid, and I bent over backwards for him.

Then I found out he was talking to girls online again, and even then he lied to me about it. Frank was milking getting shot and had lots of females writing him to express their concern. One of them tried to be my friend and so, naturally, I thought, *Finally one of his friends wants to be my friend*. We would text and video chat, and we got along great until I had Frank show me his Facebook messages.

At three or four in the morning, I happened to catch them subtly messaging each other: "Akira would be so mad if she found out," she had typed, and Frank responded, "Yeah, she would!"

My heart dropped to the floor and tears filled my eyes. I started cussing and yelling about how I hated him and how stupid I was for believing anything he ever said. I was the one taking care of him even when we weren't married.

He said, "The army is paying you to take care of me, so you can't really complain."

I said, "Excuse me?! Ok, that's it! I want to be on the first flight out of here." I packed my bags, but he managed to block me from leaving, so I ran to the spare room and locked the door and just cried. At that moment I regretted everything, but then he came in with his smooth talk and charm and made all the hurt melt away.

I couldn't figure out why I just let him hurt me, but now that I look back, I figured out why: He was just like my dad! Frank acted the exact same way toward me as my dad did with my bio mom, stepmom, and brothers! Frank was a lying, manipulative, controlling, temperamental boy, a younger version of my father, and it took me way too long to realize that. Up to that point, all I knew was that I needed him to love and need me.

Taking care of Frank made me feel important and special because there were all these other females who wanted him and wished they could be me. That feeling was awesome! I felt like for once I'd met a guy I really did love, and it wouldn't be a problem to get past his flaws and mistakes. When we were good, we were great!

Whenever Akira said something like that, it would confuse and sicken me. How could she take the scraps that Frank gave her and call them great? But she took whatever good she could get and quickly forgave the rest.

I thought of times I had seen other people do this and remembered traveling to countries whose people experienced heavy trauma and deprivation. Little things became very important to some of the survivors (e.g. certain objects, words or rituals that were connected to the past, their personal value, or their hope), and I wondered if this was similar to Akira's experience. I also remembered other people I had known who repeated destructive patterns despite the harm to themselves—there was always a reason rooted in their past, and a deep belief that the pattern was their only option.

In both situations, freedom from the old patterns meant they needed to be slowly replaced by new perspectives and experiences until the latter were as powerful as the former had been. I needed to understand better what kept Akira from being able to break from her husband. I received more than I expected when I asked, "Why did you stay with your husband when he was treating you so badly?"

I expected Frank to treat me like my dad because that's what I knew and that's what I was comfortable with. I let him control and mistreat me because I was in love with him and he was so good at manipulating me. I never stopped to think, "My dad was like this and that's why you left his house, so why would you want to be with someone like him?" All I saw was love, safety, security, and stability. I think being controlled was wrapped up in those things. I thought I had to have someone to depend on because that was all I knew how to do. Also, part of it was that I had always wanted to get married. I blame my bio mom for that. When I was thirteen, she told me, "You're gonna be just like me! You're gonna have a baby at fifteen and get married and then have more babies so you can be just like your mom." She kept saying things like that to me, and so that's honestly what I thought was going to happen.

The opportunity to get married was in front of me with Frank and I loved him. He seemed good to me, for the most part, and I wanted the stability because I had felt lost since the day I moved out of my dad's house when I was eighteen. My dad had made me so dependent on him that I knew nothing about being an adult or having responsibility. I depended on him to tell me how to walk, talk, eat, dress, and have friends. I had absolutely no social life; only one friend was okay for me to hang out with from about fifth grade until I graduated from high school. No extracurricular activities were allowed, no school games or dances. I missed out on everything and I never had a choice about anything in my life.

So when I went out into the real world, I failed miserably. I dropped out of college and partied for almost an entire year. I couldn't keep a job because I'd start one and then wouldn't like it, or partied so hard the night before that I wouldn't show up. During that time, I lived with my older brother's ex-girlfriend, who became a sister to me. She guided me and basically took care of me.

After that, I moved from house to house, couch to couch, and to friends' apartments in California. The last people I lived with in California were an older couple from my church who rented me a room. I had a curfew and I absolutely had to go to church no matter what. They said, "You are not allowed to have gay friends."

I said, "I pay you guys rent for a room, so you really have no right to set rules on me or tell me who I can or can't be friends with. If I wanted to live like this I would just move back to my dad's house!" That didn't go over well and they kicked me out. I had a day to move and nowhere to go. I called my younger brother who was stationed at Fort Drum, New York and told him I had no place to go, so he bought me a plane ticket to fly me out. That's where I met Frank.

My dad would beat the hell out of us and leave bleeding welts on our backs and butts, but then he'd feel so bad about it. He'd cry and say how sorry he was. Seeing my big, strong, tough dad crying on his knees broke my heart every time. It was hard to be mad at him and easy to forgive him, so that was the cycle.

Same thing with Frank. I was so used to the cycle that I could be thinking, "He really hurt me! I'm so unhappy, and I need to leave him because this is not a marriage, and this is not how I want to live." But then he'd do something nice, and a switch would flip inside me. Then I'd think, "This isn't so bad. It'll get better. My husband didn't mean to throw me over the couch in a jealous rage; he still loves me and takes care of me. He gives me food, a roof over my head, and stability. The least I can do is listen to him, have his uniforms ready, and make meals for him. I'm not working and I'm a wife, so I don't have the right to have an opinion on anything. I just need to listen more and stop arguing, since he's the one who puts food in the house. He is my husband and I need to respect and honor him."

I blame my stepmom for those thoughts. She was my main example for how to be a wife. She and my dad got together soon after she came to the States from El Salvador and we lived out in the orchard fields. She used to tell me that my dad would take her out there and beat her, about how angry he'd get if she didn't want to have sex with him. She'd wake up at dawn to iron his work clothes, have his breakfast waiting on the table, and lunch packed in his lunch pail.

My bio mom wasn't much help either. My dad beat her too, and she'd escape into her own little world while he was at work. I remember her sitting on the couch in the morning with her coffee and cigarette, all three of us little ones in the house, and she would be on the phone with her friends for hours. She locked the food pantry so that we couldn't get into it.

I give her props though for getting the strength to leave with my two brothers and me in the middle of the night because she couldn't handle us getting abused anymore after twelve years. The breaking point for her was when my older brother got whipped with an extension cord on the stairs, hearing the way he was yelling and screaming in pain. That night she waited until my dad went to bed, and then she loaded us in the car and drove all night to my grandpa's house.

My bio mom had the best intentions for us, but even after we moved out she just partied all the time and was gone day and night. One day my step-grandma called my dad to tell him where we were and that he needed to pick us up because our mother was not capable of taking care of us, and neither could she and my grandpa. My dad showed up a few hours later with toys in his trunk for us and tears streaming down his face because he was so happy to have us back. But it wasn't long before the abuse started again. So you see, I never had a good role model to show me how a man should treat me, how to set boundaries, how to relate with a man so that I'm not just bowing down to him.

It was clear now that Akira's mind and body had been wired for these power games, for living under the thumb of others rather than standing on her own strength, and for the turbulence of fragile men. She needed new, healthy experiences, and fortunately she had some with her aunt and uncle's family. What more was needed? Perhaps understanding her first steps out of the unhealthy pattern could illuminate what further steps were needed. "It seems like a jail where you can't even see the bars," I said. "How did you get out?"

It literally took having a child to open my eyes. I didn't want Devon growing up in the kind of household we had with Frank. I didn't want him to see me get hit and I didn't want him to get hit. When Devon was only one year old, he saw Frank and me fighting and he freaked out, trying to protect me. He was not okay with men, because he associated them with yelling and fighting. It was destroying my son to keep the family together. I wanted a better life for us, and if that meant breaking up my family, then that is what I would do.

I grew up in a broken family, and I always said I'd never do that. But I realized for Devon to grow up in an unhealthy, unhappy, angry house would be worse! Devon and I saved each other, and now we have each other. I got him out just in the nick of time, so he didn't have to see too much negativity. Now I have one happy boy!

How many men have you known in your whole life that you could trust?

What do you mean?

Men you could let your guard down with, be yourself with, talk about whatever with, and not worry.

Zero.

Okay, let's make sure. Look at your family, friends, anyone . . .

Well, kind of my uncle, but I couldn't just sit and talk with him easily. We don't have much in common. He keeps to himself. Oh, and you.

What about me?

I can do all of those things with you.

Are you saying I am the only man you can trust and let your guard down with?

Yes.

That's great and I am very glad, but you need more than me.

I know I do, but I don't know how. Right now, I just say no when guys try to talk with me or take me out. Even with you, I still have to get used to things being different. You know when you said that you would change your schedule so we could meet? The way you said it would normally be what a guy would say to flirt with me. I know you didn't mean it that way, but I had to think about it and see that you were just trying to show that I was important enough to change your schedule for.

Ok, let's find out how you came to trust me so that you can have a way to do it with other men who deserve your trust.

That sounds great. I want to do that.

What does a woman do when there is a man-sized hole inside her that blocks good relationships? What I often hear is that a chaotic something is better than a hollow nothing in the shape of what was lost—a reminder of a longing that is not being filled.

If healthy relationships are necessary for wellbeing, then a new connection may need be forged in order to break an old connection. Akira looks like and operates as an adult woman, and in many ways she is mature beyond her years because of what she has experienced. However, she has a void in her experiences regarding how to relate in a healthy way to men, how to parent, and how to believe in her dignity, worth, and competence. In these ways, she has had to learn the lessons meant to be learned as a child. She has to keep finding evidence that reveals the ideas she's accepted about herself, her gender, and her place in this world to be false—that there is another way.

This is the road she is on now. She recently received a higher paying job, has a promising guy in her life, and is parenting in more peaceful ways which she never experienced herself. She's often tempted to return to the old familiar patterns, but these temptations succeed less and less, and when they do, they bring renewed awareness of how much better her life is now.

Deadly Charm—Analysis

Summary

A woman who was surrounded by abusive and enabling people through young adulthood does not know how to function in life. She tries to find people she can trust, but their ways are confusing for her. As she reaches for independence and proving her abusers wrong, she struggles to find what she does not know.

The Trap

"I am loaded with expectations to be an adult in the world, but I don't have the skills, self-understanding, or confidence I need. They were not given to me. Many people want to manipulate me, isolate me, and leave me desperately holding onto the only supports I have known—broken ones that always crumble in the end. I discover beliefs that were fed into me that keep me weak and force me to expect failure. I fear that I do not and never will deserve what I need to be happy."

THE WAY OUT

Not Given, Not Had

- The effects of neglect are often hard to see from the inside or outside.

- Missing skills and inexperience ("experience poverty") require building on existing, related skills and experiences in order to enter the unknown.

- You don't know what you don't know, and you can't see what you can't see. Empathy and real understanding of the current state of things can lead to awareness of what is unknown and unseen.

Be a Bridge

- The counselor may need to be an exemplar, a demonstrator, a real human to practice being with and relating to, in order to find the way forward.

- You can't go off the tracks without something good to get you there. Weaknesses and failures are often linked to unseen strengths which keep them going.

- An atrophied strength requires safe initial use during the "shaky first steps" to acquire the confidence for new hope, new trust, new understanding, and new accomplishments.

★

During this break from the interviewers, I decide I need to determine if I am okay with what is happening here. This is not what I had signed up for. I had taken the advice of my editor to build the connections I need to promote my book. She thought I should take the interview, and so I did. But this is definitely more like going down the rabbit hole or taking the Matrix red pill . . . something else is going on that I am being kept from understanding. I decide that I will no longer comply with the assumption that my hosts have good intentions under their strange methods.

*When **three** interviewers enter the room this time, I feel a little intimidated. My first thought is, "Now they're bringing out the big guns." I almost let the moment go by, but instead I say, "Hey, I'm feeling uncomfortable with what's going on here. Can you answer a few questions?"*

The newest of the group, a large Hispanic man with warm, welcoming eyes, speaks first as all three sit down: "Eric. You often expect people who come to meet with you to extend trust to you without knowing what you will be entering into together. Would you be willing to trust your intuition about us and save your questions until a later time? We have good reasons for our slow disclosure."

This response surprises me. I had thought my charming request for more information would simply be met. Also, they seem to know me a little more than I feel comfortable with. Despite all this, something about this man's voice, how I experience him as I look into his eyes, makes me say, "Okay."

The now expected page is placed on the table. I name the new man Bunsen because of his warmth (like a Bunsen burner in chemistry class), and hope I can tell him sometime because it might make him laugh.

(**Bunsen**) Isn't the *Not Given, Not Had* principle obvious to know and obvious to fix? If you aren't given something you need, can't you just go get it someplace else?

(Eric) It's not as obvious as you might think. For example, the research into early development is very clear that abuse and neglect in childhood orients the brain's operation more toward survival and less toward growth. When this happens frequently enough, development can be delayed and missing skills can be glossed over. As one advances in school and expectations for more maturity pile on, young people in this situation learn to fake, hide, distract, and cover up to avoid being revealed as "not good enough." An organization in Boston called Think Kids identified many of these hidden "thinking skills" which often torment young people. They can't identify or ask for what is missing because they have never experienced it fully.

When Akira told me that I was the first man she had been able to really trust, I was struck by how many missing skills were hidden behind that statement. How does she know who to trust? What kinds of influences will she expose her son to? What ideas about masculinity will she raise him with if she doesn't have a clear idea of what a good man is?

Once you know what's missing, it's still challenging to fill it in later. She has formed habits that require her to skip steps and keep weaknesses hidden. What does a young woman in her late twenties do to experience being parented in a healthy way when she is now an adult? How does she learn to parent her son better than she had been parented? It is not easy for a single mother to find and invite safe men into her life to be mentors or friends. Unless she's part of a community where she can practice relating to safe men, she will tend to be more comfortable with what she knows—unsafe or wounded men with whom she knows her role. Kind or trustworthy guys could make her feel awkward or even repulsed.

(**Bunsen**) So this brings up another theme I keep hearing. On the one hand you seem to be honoring innocence, and on the other pointing out the problem with missing skills. Isn't innocence at a certain age just ignorance? It's fine in a child, but in stressful situations, don't we want people who are competent and good?

(*Eric*) Innocence can be protective—not knowing can be a shield, or it can hold a person captive. Often people who perform well in challenging conditions have learned how to not know as much as how to know. They have to practice what not to focus on during their vital tasks and what not to do outside their work which might diminish their potential.

Innocence can also reflect what is missing. The saying "you cannot know what you have not been given" comes to my mind when I find a missing skill or perspective a person has not had a chance to receive. Akira's story demonstrates for me that basic relationship skills were never given to her, yet she has been expected to possess them. She often repeated patterns that *obviously* didn't work to an outsider who saw these patterns, but were not obvious to her. She demonstrated obtaining this power when she told her story for the first time and saw the patterns for herself. She was operating in a less mature pattern until she had the perspective to see herself and her circumstances differently and then have new choices available.

(**Cross**) Okay, so a person doesn't get some knowledge or skill they need. How are they going to get it? You aren't saying we should leave them in that state so they can be sweetly ignorant, right?

(Eric) Let me tackle the first question because the second one might take a while. One of the best ways I have seen to reveal and break old patterns, revealing missing skills or understanding, is for a person to live temporarily with a healthy family or in a context which is not their own. Experiencing different ways of life and relating is so much more powerful than talking about it or learning it in a class. When my wife lived with some family friends for two years as a teen, it transformed her view of many parts of life which were different from her dysfunctional family of origin.

Another way is to create the space and conditions for a person to notice other options and take small steps to explore them. Generally, things like anger management and social skills groups seem crazy to me because they force people to focus on their areas of weakness. This tends to give too much energy to the weakness. A team I worked with created a disk golf group which allowed people struggling with social skills to try social encounters while focusing on a game they enjoyed, and the effectiveness was much higher. They could imagine they were coming just to play disk golf and feel good about being there, instead of coming to work on their weaknesses, which would be draining from the start.

One reason I do not easily recommend mental health professionals to use methods like this, though, is that innocence can be vulnerable to inadvertent harm. It's too easy for us to play the experts and take away potential for others. My daughter keeps this in my mind every day.

Recently she listened to a story that evoked disturbing emotions inside her. I was tempted to "fix it for her" and reduce her pain, but she didn't want me to (which was a good thing that I couldn't see in the moment). She didn't know how to talk about these emotions, so she tried to find words on the internet which described them. Eventually she landed on "disturbing emotions" and "treatment." Somehow, she found an article about lullabies being used to calm people and selected one for herself to sing. She felt better and then came to me to report, "Hey Dad, who knew treatment could be so fun?" Her sweet heart and mind mapped a course that fit what she needed with very limited guidance from us. What a pleasure to see growth and effort from many years of work build up to such a lovely moment.

(*Cross*) Perhaps this would be pursuing growth without force? Where our expectations don't get in the way?

(*Eric*) Yes. That's what makes it so tricky. We all have expectations. When we think we know something, it's natural to try to share it. However, it's easy for our expectations of a person to be set by what is normal for us, because we can't imagine a different way and can't see the capacity which is missing or hidden. More importantly, we often can't see the hidden strengths that have formed to mitigate the missing ones. When these treasures are discovered, they can first appear awkward, but freshly found strength or beauty can be amazingly untainted. I often learn a great deal from new hope, new understanding, and new potential because it is not limited by experiences that cover them up. Akira came out of a lifetime of oppression, and what she discovered were often "innocent" lessons that I have used in many future situations.

Sometimes I have to use myself as the new experience for a woman who does not know that relating to a good man is possible (or that one even exists), but it's better if she can find one as a regular part of her life.

(*Ebony*) It isn't fair! I don't like Akira's story. She seems set up for more pain, and she'll play catch-up for the rest of her life.

(*Cross*) She cannot have what she has never been given... Reminds me of "we love because we were first loved."

(*Eric*) Akira's life is an invitation to the people around her to rise up and unlock the gifts she carries. She will do this for herself, but she can't do it alone.

(*Ebony*) You paint this picture as if there's some kind of standard behind everything that anyone can reach for and have a better life. I can't find that. Truth and lies blend so often I lose what is real. Feelings often suck and I wish I didn't have them because I don't like to be hurt. I try to be stronger and stronger so no one can hurt me, but it happens anyway. I make my own cage and then I'm angry that I'm inside it. Maybe that's why some of these stories make me mad ... Can you make it clear what is inside these women that makes them step into freedom with some protection against constant pain?

(*Eric*) You just did what is required to start. You are angry but also tender in telling us about yourself and how these stories are affecting you. Would you be any stronger if you had kept that inside? We need to see both sides of you in order to be with you in it—the protective anger from past disrespect and the tender openness that allows you to connect with these women and to us.

Many of the women in these stories have uncommon potential

that was held back by core lies that deceived them into a limited expression of their life and strengths. Why? In part because they all are sensitive—capable of caring and sensing deeply. They each yearned for freedom outside their cage and yet remained trapped. Each had uncommon gifts—awareness, compassion, strong empathy, honesty, and innocence despite encounters with dark experiences and harsh limitations from people who were supposed to love them or be in their care.

One trap that often holds back uncommon people is that their strengths have "gone off the tracks." They don't know what their strengths are or how to use them, so these qualities become caught in cycles that make the strength appear to be a weakness. Sensitivity is one of these. Because a sensitive person is more likely to be hurt or reactive, they are often seen as the source of the problem. The reality is that a person with sensitivity can "see" things that other people cannot. These inner reactions are not simply emotions out of nowhere. They are messages regarding a specific stimulus or situation. They are an insight waiting to happen if the message is understood. This takes some discernment, but with help, what was "driving a person crazy" can be used to help many people.

I have often found people with clearly diagnosed psychological disorders can experience them very differently if the person who bears them understands this principle: *You cannot go off the tracks without something good to get you there.* There is always something good behind every fear, depression, or anxiety.

(*Cross*) I know you aren't saying fear, depression, or anxiety are good . . . just what's behind them. That's a fine-sounding idea, but do you have anything that I can bring back to my people which is more like a practice? The kind of thinking that makes us resist differences or unpleasant emotions seems deeply entrenched.

(Eric) One exercise that is surprisingly simple and yet often effective is called Three Steps Out. *[For a more complete form of this practice, see Appendix B.]* This exercise begins with the recognition that all emotions occur because of caring about something, that you value what you care about, and that recognizing what you value is critical to finding peace in challenging situations.

Since our brain narrows our focus and seeks similarities to threats from past experiences, we have to retrain our brains to think in specifics in order to lower our guard to a level that fits current reality. To do this, we have to **name the emotion** and to be specific about it. For example, rather than saying, "People drive me crazy—they don't get me," it would be more accurate to say, "I'm afraid of being misunderstood and hurt by people."

The second step is to *find the good behind the emotion*. Every emotion has good within it. There is no such thing as a bad emotion. We can appreciate and use our emotions productively if we pause to find the good behind what may feel like a "bad" emotion. If we understand emotions as messengers and know that they will often go away when we've received the message, we can separate ourselves from them rather than identifying with them. So in our example, the good behind my emotion is, "I want to be understood so I can have good relationships."

The third step is to **take one small step into the good**: "I'm going to choose a person I want to be closer to and share one new thing with them." Patterned, repeated behavior (or practices) toward what is good for us (or what we truly want) is the key to mental and emotional health. Keeping it fun and lighthearted, like a game, will increase our chances of being intrigued and interested instead of forced.

(*Bunsen—chuckling*) It's about time you got practical.

As the interviewers stand to leave, I wonder why we have to stop after each story. I wonder if I'm being stupid in giving these people, who clearly have some kind of agenda, the details of what I have been working so long to write about. Should I protest or quit?

    Bunsen seems to see what I am feeling and pauses to look at me.

"Eric. Everyone here shares an interest in wisdom. Your practice of reciprocal dignity is new to us and we need to have multiple people from our group experience different aspects of it. We are trying to determine whether it will fit our effort to integrate some wisdom-gathering practices into a shared compilation.

    "The small symbols we are sharing with you are ways for us to learn about how you might receive us without our assumptions getting in the way. Would you please make an attempt to integrate the symbols you are noticing into your concept of wisdom? At the end of the interviews, I promise we will tell you more about our purpose and let you decide what to do with these transcripts. Is that enough for now?"

    "Am I allowed to know your name?"

    "No. Not at this time. Perhaps on another occasion."

    "What would happen if I quit now?"

"We would give you a copy of the interview transcript so far and you would go home. We wouldn't publish anything, and you wouldn't know more."

Ebony, Cross, and Bunsen smile in a way that shows some sympathy and understanding about what I am feeling. In the end, my curiosity and gut win over my skeptical mind. I throw up my hands and grin a little as if defeated, and they nod, smile warmly, and head toward the door.

I review what I know in case I can throw a last question or comment at them before they leave. I look at the napkin eye, the triquetra tattoo, and around the room for anything I might have missed—some new connection. Bunsen's back is to me and I am struck again by him. He is obviously a bodybuilder, and I can see his tank top straining to cover his muscles. As he walks through the door, I see the phrase "Hot Sauce Walkin'" on the back of his shirt. I laugh. Why is Bunsen such a warm guy? It's like he has built up all this friendly energy and it just pours out. I notice a big scar and some burn marks on his legs as he walks away. It makes me wonder if this warmth did not come easily. When he talks to me or looks at me, I feel really seen and enjoyed. It's as if distractions or self-focus that might tie up other people affect him less. He seems intelligent and disciplined as well. This combination re-minds me of a Fyodor Dostoevsky quote: "It takes something more than intel-ligence to act intelligently." What is the "more"? It's as if wisdom has changed Bunsen in all parts of who he is—his mind is different, his body is different, his heart is different because of what he has received. It strikes me suddenly that we must embody wisdom! It's not intellectual content or pithy phrases. It's not just in the head! It must be integrally part of a being. Just like "there is no such thing as a wise and evil king," goodness is a part of wisdom and must be part of the wisdom bearer's presence.

New levels of meaning open in the stories I've been telling. These women had to see and accept their full value in order to unlock their wisdom—physical, emotional, spiritual . . . their full presence. The denial of who they were and what was inside of them somehow blocked us all from wisdom they already had. Denying themselves—their emotions, their value, their goodness—blocked certain kinds of seeing that they needed.

A high degree of stress focused their minds on survival which, over time, created protective patterns that blocked good things from coming in.

When, in our relationship, they felt seen, known, understood, accepted, and genuinely cared for, they could lift these denials or protections so that the good that was in them could come out and the good around them could come in. So it would seem that reciprocal dignity is a gateway to wisdom, and wisdom opens a way to reciprocal dignity!

Was this the missing piece of the triquetra?

What is this group doing to me? It's provoking all these questions and maybe some insights . . . Is this some kind of secret society they will invite me into? Or are these people paranoid, or psychologically obsessed, or . . .?

Alright. I have no idea. I try to prepare to give the best from my next story so that if I am being evaluated for something I might want, I will be considered worthy. Sounds like something I got from a movie or book…

I shift my mind to Grace's story. She is a fellow counselor who is gifted in her work and has the capacity not only to experience inner liberation, but to analyze, notice small details, and articulate what is going on inside her as it happens. She has often given me new insights, and I hope looking at her story with this group will lead to even more.

Dear Reader,

A friend described a problem with being seen as an expert: "When I was going through a divorce because my husband was a secret alcoholic, people didn't want to believe it. They wanted me to stay on my pedestal so that they could use me for their comfort. No one wanted to help me, because it seemed to confirm that if I could fall apart, any of them could too."

If reciprocal dignity is present early in a relationship, our view of each other is often more real, more human, and more capable of riding out the storms of life. This does not mean we can trust everyone equally. Dignity does not edit people. However, a wise offering of our reality, crafted for the good of another, can end up bringing good to both parties.

It is easier to defer to or blame authority. It is harder to bear our responsibilities together with mutual respect and care. The capacity to extend dignity requires learning to honor the self we have been given and to hold it loosely.

Through his work relating to gang members in the Los Angeles area, Fr. Gregory Boyle of Homeboy Industries says we should begin "in awe of what they carry instead of in judgement of how they carry it."

E

For years mental health professionals taught people that they could be psychologically healthy without social support, that "unless you love yourself, no one else will love you." ... The truth is, you cannot love yourself unless you have been loved and are loved. The capacity to love cannot be built in isolation.
—*Bruce D. Perry*

VI

NO LOVE FOR ME, THANKS, I'M STARVING

A Dream of Wise Counsel

> *New power – where does it go? It cannot be contained – I will not be*
> *contained*
> *Shall I hurt, shall I please, shall I go a new way and leave all behind?*
> *I break away and find solid ground,*
> *I look back and find I have more than I believed possible.*

(Eric) I met Grace through a friend shortly after moving to Colorado. We connected easily on many topics (wisdom, warm versus cold counseling, freeing women to be strong without shame), and she offered to let me share office space with her. After a few months, she extended another significant portion of trust to me by asking me to meet with her niece who was leaving an abusive situation to join her family. Her niece needed to talk with a man she could trust to process the struggles she'd been through. As I helped her adapt to independence and a home life that was completely different from what she was used to, I learned more about Grace's family.

Two months later, Grace was offered a "dream situation" where she could create her own job description, but she felt unsure about what she really wanted. She asked me to help her cut through the haze to gain some clarity. Our work happened over two years through in-person conversations, phone calls, and text messages.

Grace arrived at our first meeting looking tired, a little detached, and turbulent.

First week: a conversation

(**Grace**) I have to say, I was aware as I drove here that I have similar emotions every time I even think about talking about this stuff: I'm easily confused and end up frozen, unable to make decisions about what I want to do, what I am good at, or how I fit into the nonprofit. I felt like turning around and driving home, not because I don't want to talk with you, but because I'm aware these feelings freeze me up. I need help with these weird reservations I have about clearly stating what leadership role I'd like to take with this organization. There's something getting in the way.

Do you have a hard time receiving good things?

That's a big question. I have no idea how to answer that. Let me think . . . I don't think I have a hard time because I've had a lot of good things happen in my life, but I guess I don't really know. All that comes to mind is my early life story.

I am adopted. My biological mother has struggled with mental illness and homelessness most of her life. My biological sister, who is two years older than me, has issues with drug use and mental illness, and she has chosen homelessness as a way of life. I feel like my sister hated me for a long time for the good life I have.

Sometimes, I feel like I'm not even supposed to be alive. I was left on the doorstep of a pastor and his wife at one week old. At nine months old, I was taken in by a loving family who eventually chose to adopt me. I was often told that I was special, and I partly believed that I was the most loved person in my family. Sometimes I wonder why my sister didn't get to have a good family, too.

Can you think of other times when a good thing made you uncomfortable?

Actually, I do remember having a powerful and confusing experience after living in another country for two years with my family and the family of a dear friend. It was a meaningful experience for all of us, but as I spoke to my friend about it later, I wept. "This was such a gift. I feel like this was one of the best times of my whole life," I told her. "And also like I will never get something like this again. Our turn is over." I don't really know why I felt that so strongly.

Sometimes, after something good happens, I feel like I've had my share and probably shouldn't get any more. I feel like God is the good parent saying, "Grace, let everyone else have a first helping before you go for seconds." I feel like He's right, and yet I feel scared and sad that I won't ever have that good thing again. But good things do keep happening, and I guess I'm questioning whether I should be taking these extra helpings. I have a good husband and good children, and I have received love from parents and mentors. Why should I keep getting more?

It seems like you have a strong sense of justice that is violated by all the good things you get as you watch your mother and sister not get those things. How can God be so unfair? How can you keep taking when they don't have enough? It sounds similar to survivor's guilt experienced by soldiers and people who have lived through death or tragedy.

I've never known why, but I've always been obsessed with stories about survivors and tragedies. Plane crashes, orphan and poverty stories—I'm always curious about those who struggle with extreme circumstances or what happens to the survivors of catastrophes.

Maybe you limit what you are allowed to enjoy so that you can tolerate your uncomfortable sense of "unjust receiving".

Say that again . . . unjust receiving? Okay, I'm not even sure what that means. As we're talking, I'm feeling something scary inside. Do you think this really has to do with why I feel stuck about this job description stuff? Are you sure you want to talk about this with me?

It's really up to you, but I'm ready to keep going, and it does feel like we've found something important.

Second week: a conversation

I just went to a Richard Rohr conference on the Trinity. He talked about how there's an infinitely rich relationship between all three parts of God, and that I am welcome into this relationship, to receive from the abundance there. I want to. I know with my mind that I'm able to receive unlimited grace, but I feel like I have received my due already. When I remember my biological mom and her fragileness, when I think about my sister in her suffering, I see a connection—they are unseen, overlooked. So many experiences trigger my discomfort. Any disparity—like seeing a person who is homeless or someone who is wealthy—makes me think, "That's not right!" I am realizing that I carry a sense that *I am not right,* that I am "white trash." I am embarrassed at what I am, but not embarrassed by my mother and sister. I see the value in them. I am bothered by how other people are bothered by them. I am ashamed about the part of us that is seen as trash. I try to hide that part of myself.

How can I accept that my mother has a severe mental illness and that she abandoned my sister and me to the system? Why have they spent many years homeless and abused when I have been given so much? Isn't it wrong for me to get so much when they get so little?

I wonder if there is a part of you that doesn't want to be free. If you are free, then it might feel like you're prideful and unjust, forgetting or dishonoring the pain of your sister and mom.

I have to pay for my life and the "too much good" I have already received. I have to be ready for the good to end. I feel like God will eventually say, "It's other people's turn."

This definitely sounds like survivor's guilt. You can't reconcile their pain with your good. You try to balance things out by working hard to rescue people and by giving yourself away. You deny yourself good things and doubt the truth and security of what you have. You receive your sister's anger and believe it is justified. You live believing your mother left you for good reason, and now you doubt your worth. You operate as if you shouldn't be loved.

I have noticed I expect similar things in my current family. My kids must be grateful or they're in big trouble. It's as if I'm saying, "You'd better appreciate what you don't deserve. Don't ask for second helpings. Sit down and be good!" In my current relationships, I can withstand a lot of not being cared for and doing more than my share of the work, because I'm used to the imbalance.

So you're stuck in an environment of unending struggle between trying to create justice and not receiving it yourself. Does that make you feel angry?

I know this is important, but I think I need to let that soak in for a while. Can we talk about that more next time?

A text message

This quote by John O'Donohue really resonates with me right now, because you challenged me to allow myself to feel anger:

> *Awaken to the mystery of being here*
> *And enter the quiet immensity of your own presence.*
> *Have joy and peace in the temple of your own senses.*
> *Receive encouragement when new frontiers beckon.*
> *Respond to the call of your gift and the courage to follow its path.*
> *Let the flame of anger free you of all falsity.*
> *May warmth of heart keep your presence aflame.*
> *May anxiety never linger about you.*
> *May your outer dignity mirror an inner dignity of soul.*

Take time to celebrate the quiet miracles that seek no attention.
Be consoled in the secret symmetry of your soul.
May you experience each day as a sacred gift woven around the heart
   of wonder.

A text dialogue

A friend confronted me today and said that I'm a hard person to disappoint. I think she could tell that when I'm hurt by something in a friendship, it brings me down further than it should. When things like that happen, I feel anger at being misunderstood. I hide my anger because I know it will be disruptive and might make me lose my relationship, or at least create distance. I just go home and want to hide or sleep, and then I feel guilty. My needs get lost.

It seems like you work very hard to keep all your friendships going. You don't rest in them and fully enjoy them. You hold them together by acting how you're supposed to—always giving more than you allow yourself to receive. You must be there for them. When your needs are known, you're scared it will ruin things, that they will be too much for anyone to handle. They might reveal that they don't really want to be with you.

How can I trust in the love of my friends? It took me a long time to accept the love of my adopted mom. I only let her love me two years before she died. How can I let others in who might do the same? When I let someone love me, then the love will end up going away. I feel like I have to hold it all together, but I get tired from it all.

An email

This is really resonating with me from the Enneagram (an assessment model of the human psyche). I'm a type Eight:

> *Type Eight: The Need to Be Strong:* The Eight's primal know-
> ing was that God/Reality was warmth, food, protection,
> empathy, relationship, and total understanding of how weak,
> needy, and hungry we all are. Feeling separate from such a
> nurturing God leaves the Eight vulnerable and needy. To
> seemingly "fix" this dilemma, the Eight's ego decides to hate,
> reject, deny, and project that neediness everywhere else—so
> they don't have to cry over it inside themselves. "I will never
> cry," they say, and "I will protect the little ones from crying."
> They decide to do God's work themselves...
>
> Eights do a good job of hiding their vulnerability. They im-
> press us as strong and mighty; they are capable of imparting a
> feeling of strength to others as well. They have a strong sense
> of justice and truth. They instinctively know when dishonesty
> or injustice is at work...
>
> Fortunately, Eights like to take the side of the weak. Their
> passion for justice and truth often leads them to side with the
> oppressed and defenseless. This is because they unconsciously
> know that within their own innermost self—behind a façade
> of hardness, invulnerability, curses, or even brutality—there's
> a vulnerable little boy or a little girl (which they reveal to
> very few people). When you're really poor, helpless, and weak,
> the Eight's protective instinct is aroused, and they will do

anything to assist you. But as soon as you express in any way that you have your own power, then the Eight will prove that they have more power.

Who would not love all that Eight stuff; even if it does wear you out?

A phone conversation

Eric, I'm hiding my face while I talk to you because I feel so confused and embarrassed about needing to grieve, needing to be angry about the things that've happened in my life, and then allowing someone to see these feelings. I don't fully understand, and I'm scared. I know this is good, but I feel like I'm losing everything!

Let's tackle that sense of ambivalence head on, and maybe that will help you find what's solid in your life. What is ambivalence?

I would say two different desires that are inside of me, competing— neither one ever wins. I can't ever decide what direction to go in. Isn't that kind of like a paradox?

I think they are similar. A paradox often has an inner resolution, but it doesn't look like it from the outside. It can be an invitation into the depth of seeming opposites, because when you hold them in tension, often a new way is revealed that creates unity. Ambivalence, on the other hand, hasn't found resolution. The opposites tangle each other up so neither part can have its place. Energy is wasted in maintaining a draining cycle.

I feel this every morning when I wake up—anticipating the tension. I can never work out my feelings and I can't figure out which way to go, because I have to see good where there is bad and bad where there is good. Bad things have to balance out the good; otherwise someone is being wronged.

If you can find the emotions under the ambivalence, like being scared, anxious, or angry, I think you'll find they are the clues to freedom. They tell you something about yourself. Let that truth stand, and you will see what is hidden behind the tension. It seems to me that part of the tension comes from you taking responsibility for things that are not yours. Unless everyone's pressing emotional needs are taken care of around you, you don't deserve nourishment. You have to be strong in this way, and then maybe you get to find out if their connection to you is real. This kind of caring is impossible to carry for one person, so you never get enough nourishment or reassured connection.

Since good and suffering come no matter what you do, maybe letting the uncertainty come without taking responsibility for it will allow things to balance out and give you a better place to contribute from.

A text a few days later

Because you are seeing my real way of being behind the scenes, I am starting to let go of my hidden game. I know it hasn't been working, but I have invested too much in it to see it clearly. I also feel too ashamed to change it. It's like a trust fall. What if you walk away? I feel like I am losing everything: my friends, my energy, everything I thought was true. I don't know the way forward anymore. It feels like dying. I want to run away to a different life, because if I don't come through for the people in my life, I will lose them. If I don't keep working on the unfairness around me, a sense of wrongness rises up and is almost unbearable.

You are not losing your friends. You have been holding back and are learning to truly gain them. You are not losing your energy. You thought your foundation was built on fear-based striving; you will stop doing that kind of work, stop wasting energy, and have more available. You are not losing your bearings. You were using a broken compass. Now you are getting used to a new one that works better, but it is awkward because it works differently. You are not losing what little emotional nourishment you have. You are agreeing to eat what you are used to refusing. You are learning to accept temporary injustice (getting more than your mom or sister) in order to be a participant in greater justice formation (having abundance to give away).

A text the next day

Eric, stop whatever you are doing and listen.

Your presence with me today—a gift!

I see a little crack with some light.

You see and are kind.

You get in the mud with me and are not afraid.

Thank you.

Third week: a conversation

I really think I need to see a counselor because I'm falling apart. I feel super shaky inside almost all the time—like I am being undone. I've had ways to deal with life before, but now I'm not supposed to use them anymore?

That is so important. You are changing so quickly and letting go of so much. Something very powerful is happening and you are fragile right now. It was hard for you to share what you have so far. I am concerned you might go back into a protected state if you try to start over. You can jump through any counseling hoop and pull the wool over the eyes of any counselor if you don't feel comfortable—you may not believe that they really care. I'm not sure taking what you're going through to a person operating as a therapist is going to work for you right now. You can meet with me as a counselor, if you want.

But I think I need your friendship right now. I seriously don't want to lose that by entering into a counseling relationship, but I also need the structure and predictability, so I'm not sure what to do. I want to submit myself to direction, and I need a safe space to allow someone to see me, and I need enough trust to receive it.

I'm guessing you need to know someone really cares about you and that the relationship is authentic.

I need to know that the person wants to be there, that they can show me that this stuff is actually worth dealing with, that I am worth dealing with, and that it's more than paid listening and reflecting. I need some awareness of all this that I don't already have.

I've done both roles before—friend and guide—and I know how to make it work. This need is one reason why I can't become a licensed counselor under the medical system. I operate as a consultant so I can have the freedom to do things like this. What would you call the person you are asking for that fits what's happening here?

Maybe you could be my PsychoBro—a friend and a counselor. I'm scared to lose our friendship, but I will trust you and try it.

We'll figure out the parameters around how we meet and communicate . . . it can work if you think about it and decide that it does fit you.

Fourth week: a conversation

I talked with my husband about the decision to meet with you regularly while keeping our friendship, and he agrees with you and thinks we should go ahead. That helps, but I'm feeling a lot of ambivalence again. I'm trying to have a more genuine relationship with my friends by telling them what's happening to me and explaining what I am doing with you, but it's very uncomfortable. I don't want it questioned, ruined, or misunderstood. It feels hard to explain. I'm a little scared people will misunderstand or cast a shadow over something that I feel is so good. I did talk to my husband about this part too, and he feels it is worth it and that we should continue to meet.

This fear seems like so many things in your life. You are transforming! You're letting go of what wasn't really working. It was familiar and kind of worked, but really it kept you restricted and hidden. It's hard to imagine life without controlling how people see you. You are a gifted counselor, and your perceptive and adaptive strengths make hiding and controlling possible, but it also holds you back from life.

Sometimes I feel like I am an eleven- or twelve-year-old girl who is stubborn and won't take what's good for her. She just won't go to the table God set in abundance, and nothing will make her go. This girl . . . I'm so frustrated with her! I can't comfort her or empathize with her. She's hungry and everyone knows it, but she pretends like she doesn't need anything. Why won't she just sit at the table and eat? I'm sick of her just sitting there in the back of the room. She should knock it off!

What's happening near the table is unjust. You'd never allow this to happen to anyone else; you'd never accept a girl starving while food was nearby. Why is it different with you as the little girl? What holds her back is the lie that she isn't allowed at the table, that she can't eat the food in front of her, that she can't be hungry in front of others. You believe that lie, but are mad at her for believing it. What I am moved by right now is that you are doing the opposite with me. You allowed me to meet this sweet little girl that you would prefer to keep hidden. You are allowing yourself to need in front of me—that is brave.

An email

Eric, I have been struggling with this idea of receiving goodness and being hungry. I wrote this to try to express what is inside me:

> Five foods. I'm starving. I didn't know it but I am. Shaking, hollow, groans, and headaches I guess were always what I thought were normal. Weird. I've always had enough to keep living, but for some reason when I was offered something "real" to eat, say a ripe avocado or a bowl of hot steel-cut oats with honey, I would give a simple gesture of dismissal, "Eh . . . I'm good." This became so routine, I didn't even think twice as I went on my weak, gaunt way. *I'm hungry* are words never uttered, and yet the scraps of meat and crumbs of bread I found in the dirt path in front of me seemed fine to pick up, or the leftovers someone was gonna throw away anyway would suffice. "I'm good," and off I went.

> A rich, warm, decorated dark chocolate cake topped with a

large scoop of vanilla bean ice cream and five lines of buttery caramel drizzled on top . . . I couldn't, not while my sister walking next to me has anorexia. 'Tain't right. 'Tain't proper. I wouldn't want to be greedy. Later maybe, when all are in bed I can come back down, get on all fours, and wipe the floor clean of the frosting, crumbs, and drips of milk left over from the party, and I can be all good knowing I'm not hungry.

If I were left on a deserted island with nothing but five foods of my choice, love, peace, joy, memories of my most loved, and imagination would make a daily feast. I only hope I can unabashedly pull my chair up to the table and know that "I'm hungry." Thank God for food. Give me this day my daily bread. I receive. I hope I don't have to be stranded in order to come to the table.

Fifth week: a conversation

I don't like my own story. I used to have a good one, and now I don't. I was the victorious adopted girl who was strong. I had hard things in my past, but they helped me show that I overcame adversity to become someone who was respected, who helped other people. Now we both know the truth that a lot of my life is broken—that I am often depressed and depleted. I feel and do weird things in relationships. I have shame about all this, and I feel vulnerable around you.

Through these conversations, I am remembering old parts of my story that I hid or glossed over. When I was five to ten years old, I wanted to be a boy. I would insist on wearing jeans all the time, and they had to have pockets in the back. Before and after I hit puberty, I desperately and aggressively sought closeness with boys and men without considering the means I used to get it. Why? Couldn't someone have helped me see myself better?

Here is how I see those things: You have been feeling for a long time that something is wrong with you, and this "flaw" is the reason you were not kept by your biological parents, nor understood by others. As a child, you thought life might be better if you were a boy. As a teen and young adult, it was less scary to take a shortcut to intimacy through sex than to show someone your real self and risk being vulnerable.

It is so hard for me not to hate myself for feeling such stupid things. I can hardly imagine the way you are describing it, that I had real reasons for doing it. I wanted closeness, and I was ashamed that I wanted it so much and that I didn't have enough. I feared I wasn't worth getting it. Isn't the fact that I'm scared of closeness proof that I am broken? I still want to cover it all up—it's hard to hope for meaning in it.

There is meaning in it! It's the key to your freedom! Your shame shows that you want others to know you and love you, and you want to be in deep relationships that are fruitful. That is a wonderful thing!

Sixth week: a conversation

Grace, let's talk about how you receive good things. I want to tell you about

something that I sense when I ask how you are and you say, "I'm good."
I have a rather strong reaction: It actually makes me feel sick. It's how I
would feel if I was witnessing tragic harm. It's like you're saying, "I will
make do." Yes, you can and probably will . . . and it will diminish your gifts
and purpose. It's as if you are saying, "I don't need any more. Give it to
others or I will feel guilty." You have to eat or you can't help others as well
as you want to.

Part of it is that I don't want anyone to see me as greedy, especially when you've already given me so much. I've been thinking a lot
about not being able to receive what's good for me, and I know now
I have mistakenly believed my existence isn't good. Very early in my
life, I was not given important physical experiences of nurture, and
it has left a deep doubt regarding my being—like I have to prove it
every day. The insecurity and shame are so deeply embedded in me. If
I step out of my protections—being strong and needing nothing—I'll
be revealed as a scared, small person in need of endless affirmation. I
hate being like that!

It's clear to me that even your suffering is shaping something good in you.
Our talks have inspired me to write a little story about how you struggle to
receive the gift of yourself. It's called "The Inside-Out Jacket." May I read it
to you?

> *Once there was a spunky little girl whose dad smiled at her toughness.*
> *He found a leather jacket with sharp spikes sticking out of the elbows,*
> *shoulders, chest, and arms. It was a bright color and seemed to capture*

her spirit, so he bought it for her before he had to leave on a very long trip. The gift was given without any instructions, so the girl accidentally put it on inside-out. The spikes pressed into her skin and it hurt, but it seemed like it was how the gift was supposed to be used.

Her dad returned two years later. He saw how she was wearing the jacket and was horrified. "Please take it off and wear it correctly! I would never want to you to be in such constant pain!" This request was hard for the girl because she had gotten used to the pain and wearing the jacket correctly made her feel the holes in her skin. Each hole was tender without a spike to fill it. The air blew on her skin and it made her feel pain and weakness. It even confused her as to who she was. She was a tough girl! She shouldn't feel these soft things! So she kept putting the jacket on inside-out until her father caught her and pleaded for her to wear it without pain.

Oh . . . this story resounds with something deep inside. Who am I if I don't have the spikes poking in me? I can't face people without this jacket on! I feel such discomfort without the tough persona and being so close to my wounds. People need to deal with my tough sides, and if they don't like it, too bad. The pain reminds me to be tough, and I need that toughness so that I don't need affirmation. My insecurity is bottomless! How can God ever heal this insecurity? How much affirmation does one girl need? I need someone ALL THE TIME to tell me it's okay, that I am the one who is supposed to be here.

Seventh week: a conversation

I feel like there are three parts of myself that are sometimes at war with each other. The *biker chick* (who can flip off the world and do whatever she wants), the *little girl* (who lives in a cage and is starving), and the *accomplisher* (who has to care about everything or it will all fall apart). Who am I without all these parts? Nobody! Maybe I'm flawed beyond repair. God doesn't promise to heal everything. Trying to maintain these parts drains me and leaves me with the sense that nothing really matters. Nothing is worth it. I don't get anywhere.

If you picture that seven-year-old you, the little girl, what comes up inside you?

I feel impatient and frustrated. I want to say, "Fine, just stay there—don't come out." I give her a little patience and listen for a little while to see if she will talk, but she needs to deal and get on with it. People might say, "She needs acceptance," but no I don't, F you! She deserves to be there! If you empathize with her, you help her stay there. I hate empathy and being told good things about myself because I can't know if people are telling the truth or just trying to get me to do what they want. Why do I need good things anyway?

Okay, this is important. You are blending yourself and the little girl inside you, which feels both true and confusing. The anger you're feeling now is protecting something. What is it?

Shame. I hate this stuff being inside of me. It's terrible. I just try and live like it's not there. I am NOT that girl who needs to hide . . . but I am. Ugh!

Are you ashamed of the shame?

Uhhhh. That feels super powerful to me. It makes me feel like I need someone to convince me not to hate myself, but why? I don't want to trust. It's too scary. Earlier on, you told me we should start with me so I have someone to try this risk with, and I see the wisdom in that, but I want to play the game with you too. I want to hold you at a distance. I'm scared that you will watch me run up to the same walls over and over and never get past them. You probably shouldn't have taken me on as a friend—you didn't know what you were getting into; I'm too needy and high-maintenance.

I don't see it like that. You are breaking free and will have more to give when your needs are met.

Eighth week: a conversation

Eric, you have a unique way of saying deep things very directly, simply, and clearly, but without cliché. This helps me understand my-self from a new perspective. I trust you as a friend, brother, and coun-selor. Maybe you could have gotten in with me just as a counselor, but that would have been harder because I wouldn't have believed that you cared. I approached you for help as a friend, so my guard was down, and you took a risk by asking questions that opened me up. *You got in the way.* You cared about my ambivalence, making stronger and stronger statements that cut into my defenses and opposed my game. The way you talk forced me to choose whether or not I would trust you with things I have kept hidden from myself and others my whole life. I felt undone.

I wanted many times to rally and get us back on equal footing. I shouldn't just receive! But I finally had to tell myself, "I think he re-ally cares." Even if it was just for seconds at a time, I had to trust you. I still struggle with doing that, you know. You are too kind to me, be-ing my brother and my counselor—it's out of the box. But this type of relationship has helped give me the strength to trust your care and believe that my wounds matter.

There is something I have wanted to tell you, but also really didn't want to. When I was seven years old and my sister Crystal was nine, I was sent to her house for a visit. Crystal was so excited to see me because we only saw each other twice a year. When I arrived, she was laughing and running and jumping around the house and having a hard time calming down. Her adopted mom, Anna, was not excited and quickly became frustrated with Crystal. Right there in front of me, this woman brutally beat my sister for not calming down, for be-ing excited to see me.

I shut down. I didn't know what to do. Anna locked Crystal in her room for the rest of the day. When my mother came to pick me up at the end of the day, I wouldn't sit in the front seat with her. I sat in the back, unable to speak. The only thing I said was, "I never want to go back there again." And I didn't. My mom tried to get me to talk many times after that, but I wouldn't. My mom died without ever knowing what happened. I didn't see my sister again until I was twenty-two years old.

Wow. This makes sense why your little-girl self feels like she is in a cage.

I never connected my little self with my current self. I never connected how I treated my seven-year-old self to how I treat myself now. It just seemed like me. I've felt it wasn't right to want anything. Want? Pssh! My sister's in jail! My mom is dead! It's not fair to live when they can't! This is my lot!

So how are you able to be a good counselor while struggling with all that? Doesn't it mean you have a pretty amazing gift if you can help so many people while being so trapped and depleted?

It isn't like that. As a counselor, I only affect one person at a time. I was once told, "You are wonderful—a balance of laughter and perception! People feel really known by you and enjoyed by you. You have a big heart." But I can't receive joy from that. If I am that, then I want to hide. To believe that would be too much pressure: "Now I'm going to disappoint them." I have to keep being what they think I am. I don't trust that I am those good things without striving to make them happen all the time.

This is the battle inside you. You now see it far more clearly. We need to give you the space to allow your old habits to fall away and your new way of see-ing to become normal.

A phone dialogue

Eric, you have given me some new truths:

- I already have much more than I know. I don't let my-self experience it.

- I must recognize my own beauty to see my place in the world.

- I have to allow the feeling of temporary injustice to be present in order to get to deeper justice.

- I have not felt free to express my anger at unfair things that happened to me.

That anger needs to come out to give me the strength to break out of the cage. This is all so deep, I don't know if I can change *this* much. Eric, you said you wanted to do this. Are you sure you want to keep going?

You can blame me for wanting to do this. But for all your courage to keep going and for all the times you could have quit, you have to give yourself some credit.

I don't know about that, but I'm glad not to feel like I am completely falling apart anymore. We are still friends, right?

It's too late for that to change. The friendship was solid before the "counseling" began. Nothing you tell me is going to ruin that. Nothing you tell me will be too much. It will only add depth.

I need these words—to practice hearing and trusting this in order to move forward. I need to see that you aren't frustrated or bothered by my needs. Here's a quote I found by Peter A. Levine: "Trauma is not what happens to us, but what we hold inside in the absence of an empathetic witness."

Ninth week: a conversation

Eric, all the men in my life seem to want to keep me starving. My adopted dad was emotionally unavailable and passive. He loved me, but didn't really know how to connect. I felt like he didn't want to connect with me, and I had to draw him out in order for him to see me or do anything with me. I had a pastor friend who crossed boundaries with me and allowed too much intimacy into our relationship. My husband has even more shame than I do. He only gives me the minimum because he thinks I will judge what he gives. I mean, I know I am a part of all this, but it's true that the men in my life have neglected my heart.

And then there's my mom, who is the one person I felt unconditionally loved by.

When she died, I felt like I would never be allowed to experience love again.

I had gotten up early to call my mom on my first day of college, so excited to share my new college life with her. When my dad answered, he told me she had an aneurism the night before and wasn't expected to live. I left immediately to go back home, hoping to see her one more time.

When I arrived at the hospital, she was brain dead. I climbed in bed with her and just held her. She was a gift that had been given to me by God. I was filled with feelings of gratitude and awe at what I received. I remember holding her body and then just walking away, full of her inside me. It seemed that I wasn't meant to have her for very long, so on that day I felt primarily thankfulness.

Later, though, I had to accept it: I didn't get to have any more of that kind of love. Looking back, there was no room in me to feel mad or sad, just the empty, longing space she left. I didn't deserve to have her at all. But I miss her so much. I needed her for a lot longer! Then again, I really shouldn't be upset that she's gone, because she was a gift. I mean, my sister never even had a mom who loved her. And look at what I got: unconditional love. How dare I be angry or sad about that!

My own daughter recently went to college, and now I cry and cry. It seems like it will never stop. I am now the age my mother was when she died, and my daughter is the age I was when I lost her.

You are finally mourning your mother! Whenever you've talked about her in the past, it felt to me like there was a noble shield around her—like a woman sleeping under glass. You weren't allowed to feel what you desperately needed to feel because her love had been encased.

Now that you've learned to let your cages and cold justice die, you can grieve the loss of your mother and your daughter's move at the same time. I think you couldn't grieve when she died because you didn't think you had the right to.

Two Months Later

As I learn to grieve, or let myself fall apart, I no longer spend so much time hiding my shame and sadness, and I've found that I have more energy and strength. I'm able to enter into hard relationship issues without the old pain overwhelming me, and I can let people slowly meet me where I'm at.

The last relationship I had to do this with was the hardest. My husband. If he was an evil man, it would have been much easier. He has an amazingly tender and warm heart, but ever since our honeymoon, I've felt like he's withheld significant parts of it from me. As I chased, pulled, yelled, and tried to do his emotional work for him, he grew even more distant.

But grieving the loss of my marriage (even while I was in it) and the pain hiding our struggles required allowed me to stop forcing things to happen. I began to make space for him to be where he's at, the good and the hard. He has started to come toward me in some new ways. At first, I didn't like how he did it. It was too little. It was too practical. He wouldn't come forward fully into the relationship, which felt like he was taunting me.

But I began to offer parts of myself to him gently without the overwhelming fear that he would hurt me. Somehow, we began to reconnect. It's slow, but each step lasts because we are understanding new things about each other.

I didn't know that I had blocked the very thing that I wanted—to be wanted. I didn't know I was starving. I only knew that I was depressed, confused, and stuck. But slowly I began to see and receive, though sometimes it still feels wrong.

Grace continues to see how many of her clients carry wounds like her own. At times it is hard because the client's suffering stirs up her own, but upon reflection she's able to take what she knows from her own experience and offer it back gently, sometimes piercingly, to help her clients grow.

She feels less hidden, more out, more free to be herself: "There is a place for me." Her own story can matter, can have significance. This gives her more space to receive and to give. Life has proportion—not too big, not too small. A good place to be.

Recently she sent me a text that said, "My heart is AWAKE! I want to stay awake."

No Love for Me—Analysis

Summary

A successful counselor reveals that she is driven by a deep fear that her life does not matter. All her successes and friendships seem to be held together only by her own effort—if she rests, they will all go away, revealing that she is not enough and should be dismissed. Her earliest suspicion that she does not deserve to live will be verified.

The Trap

"I used to have a heroic story, but it hid that I believed my life has been overlooked. I have always had to prove myself and my place. I can never stop giving myself to others or they will leave me and decide I should not have been with them in the first place. I run myself ragged and then collapse in depression, only to start again as soon as I have any energy to give away. I am hollow and dying every day. I want to run away. There are too many people who need me and have to believe that I am strong. I can't do it anymore. The number one goal of my life is to hide this wound and find someone who will love me."

THE WAY OUT

Reverse the Void

- Deeply held false beliefs can be like an illusory machine driving a person.

- When a fundamental void drives a person, it, and not the symptoms, must be found and dealt with.

- Whenever a person is diminished, drained, or anxious, look for twisted strengths, ambivalence, or unbalanced patterns—their resolution releases energy for other uses.

Dig For True Self, Not Dead Patterns

- Dead patterns are built on good intentions, which are connected to what the true self cares about.

- Hollow repetition and persistent confusion are traps, not true choices.

- Dead patterns are not a person's true self and can be changed, though doing so may feel like dying.

★

The door opens as if on its own and no one comes in. I see the pub is noisy and active again because the night crowd has come. Our back room has some well-designed acoustics to grant us privacy, and I am grateful. The energy of the crowd enlivens me, but I am glad to be separated from them. The lanterns are turned up to match the activity of the people. I feel love for this place.

A group is moving through the pub toward the interview room as if in a procession. They are carrying something with reverence, like at a funeral, and I assume it is a casket. They seem to be crying, but as I look closer, I am surprised. The group includes the three interviewers I've met and someone new—a very tall Asian woman—Chinese if I had to guess. They are snickering and trying to hide it! A small sign on a tiny flagpole sticks up from the head of the casket: "I'm not dead yet!"

My mouth hangs open in surprise. "What the . . . ?"

They all enter the room and close the door. A forced quiet comes as the gigglers do their best to regain composure. Then I hear a voice coming from inside the casket, an old woman's voice I think I recognize: "Eric! Can you laugh at this? Can you laugh at yourself? Can you laugh at"—

Suddenly the casket bursts open and a bright white skeleton sits up out of it! I jump back, but quickly notice one hand is giving me a thumbs up and the rib cage has a "Hello, My Name is Death" nametag stuck to it.

The entire group is dying with laughter. They are on the floor, on the table, grabbing their stomachs, leaking tears as they laugh and laugh.

"You needed this, dude!"

"You were so serious this whole time!"

"We are sooooo scary aren't we, Eric?"

"Did you see his face?"

I can't help but laugh with them even as I feel dumb. Had I been so stiff? Dang. I guess so. I had been focused so much on figuring out what was going on that I hadn't been able to just enjoy these people.

I start to feel a little sheepish. All four of them look at me as if they know I'm a little ashamed and pause to let me recover my bearings.

"We have one more surprise, but it's not quite so shocking."

"It'll help you relax."

"Bring it in!"

The door to the room opens again and I see a familiar profile come into the light.

With open arms and a welcoming spirit, an elder from my past walks toward me, saying, "Come here, dear one!"

"Becka!"

As I hug my old friend, my hands feel the back brace supporting her spine. I am struck by how much suffering she has walked through to be here with me in this moment. I step back and smile at her warm eyes, and I see the lines on her face that record decades of solitude which followed a horrific early marriage. Somehow, she walked through these storms and now has abundant crackly energy and depth. She has been a mentor to me even though she lives far from me.

"Becka! How did you get here? How are you a part of this?"

"Hi, sweet friend. Don't worry. We'll have plenty of time for that conversation later, but for now you need to know that these people found me and brought me here to help you get this project done. They want me to help you get used to a new reality that will come after you leave here. I have agreed because I know quite a few people who are a part of the group."

"Were you a part of this before I got here? How?"

"Yes and no. I didn't know that some of my old friends and students had begun working together, but I knew we shared a love of wisdom. I knew we all lamented its loss of place in our time, but I didn't know something was being done about it. I'm here to help as long as I can. I need you to let go of your questions for now so we can get done with this part. It will be worth it."

"Okay. I will. I . . . I'm glad you're here. Are you feeling okay, physically?"

"Some pain is worth it."

I scan her with more scrutiny and notice the muscles in her shoulders slightly clenching involuntarily and then releasing; her hunching forward is more pronounced, and she is working to stay relaxed. I know she doesn't want me to focus on her pain.

"Thank you, Beck . . . Wait. Where is the old woman? I heard her voice." *My mind caught up and wondered where the voice, seemingly from the coffin, had come from.*

Everyone grins, sticking their hands out with fists closed downward, and then opening them up one at a time like a bunch of synchronized cheerleaders. When the tenth hand opens, it belongs to the Chinese woman, and a little iPod-like device rests in her palm. She presses play and the voice of the old woman speaks, "Oh, Eric. We like you. You're a good sport. Can you see what's happening a bit better now? Don't worry. We're with you. Let us be with you a little more, and good will come. Sometimes we need to die a bit in order to live, don't you think?"

Such a rich, lovely voice. Each time I hear it, it's as if my chest is opened up to receive in a new way. I so want to meet her, but I understand that this is all I am going to get. The group begins to sit down preparing to ask questions.

They set the page on the table, and the tall woman (I decide to call her Minnie) nods once as if to say, "Ready?"

(*Bunsen*) Do you see why this kind of humor is important, and even related to wisdom, Eric?

(*Eric*) I'd better at this point! You are all crazy! But yes, I hear what you are saying, and it reminds me of a story. A friend once told me he traveled to Russia after the Iron Curtain came down and stood outside one of the gulags to talk with the people who were freshly released. He was immediately struck by the difference between those who looked like walking death and those who still had a burning light in their eyes, even as their bodies were tormented. He asked them, "How did you hold onto life in this place?" He told me he probably could have asked it in a better way, but he was too deeply affected. So he kept repeating the question and received many answers, but the most consistent one from those who were alive inside was "dark humor." They had learned to laugh even at the most tragic circumstances and protected themselves as they did.

(*Bunsen*) Good. Ok, back to Grace's story . . . those early imprints are so deep. How can she reverse her *Voids*?

(*Eric*) They are deep and hard to change. Deeply held false beliefs can be like a powerful engine, eventually coming to drive a person. Even though Grace had a loving adoptive mother, she couldn't let her love in until she was a young adult. She performed correctly, but she didn't know or deal with her own emptiness. She thought this was good!

(*Minnie*) Yes. Her biological parents were caught in their own traps.

They were also fighting secret, anxious battles that left them weakened enough to give up their children. It seems like these generational bondages can just go on forever! I was often not allowed a social place in my early years simply because I looked different than people expected. It created a longing within me for a place to belong, and it also created a heart for others who were left out. A difficult desire to bear, especially when exclusion is everywhere. How do you break the mental chains that block such hopes?

(Eric) The next story holds a powerful answer to that question, but I will wait until later to address that. For now, let's view people who don't fit in or are drained or anxious as having strengths that have been twisted or trapped in unbalanced patterns. The energy to hold a void or broken pattern comes from somewhere. If it's strong, it often comes from a misunderstood strength used incorrectly.

(Becka) Why do twisted strengths work so well to hold people down?

(Eric) If any of us take in too much input, we shut down, lash out, or run away. The same gifts that can make a person aware, able to sense invisible relational dynamics, or observe small nonverbal details can create an inner firestorm—making interactions with people a source of torture.

I saw raw wisdom in Grace and in the coming story about Petra. When I first met them, I saw that they had been trained to believe they were flawed. They had been drowning in their own perceptions, because they had been given destructive answers about what they were perceiving and experiencing.

It's challenging to see broader or deeper truths when less significant details scream for attention. A friend referred to the training required to do this as balancing our absolute insignificance with our vast capacity. We often hold onto small truths when larger ones are needed, or large ones when smallness is needed. I call this skill *perceiving proportion*. It frequently surprises me how the hard work needed to gain this skill can lead to peace, because it allows us to let go of the things that we were never actually holding. We let go of trying to force things that we were never really able to force. Only then can we embrace the abundance that was always there.

In these stories, the women let what they thought was true die. They were protecting themselves in ways that left them perpetually wounded and starving. They held onto important virtues like truthfulness and caring for others, but to an extent that diminished them.

I see the potential for all the women in these stories to be healers. To the degree that they have suffered, they have experience, perception, and understanding to offer to others. Each one has strengths that, when better understood, are no longer used to bind themselves up, but could be used to unbind others.

(**Cross**) I see this from the side of faith communities that often have well-intentioned leaders who aren't trained to deal with the toughest mental health situations. People who suffer with these situations often suck up the most time and energy and can really hurt people if the faith leaders don't understand what is happening. I don't think the answer is to let anyone who has an interest or heart for these things just dive in. We often don't know who to trust when a crisis hits. I wish we had a directory that was vetted for our needs, tested, and updated and included someone who could help match each person to the right provider. Couldn't you gather the best folks you can find and help them stand together and teach others? It sounds like you have had a lot of hard experiences, and standing alone in a private practice isn't a good use of what you've learned. What have you learned from your past attempts at building a good healing team?

(Eric) Building an organization from scratch is tough, especially if you're aiming for sources of funding that allow flexibility in practice. Often there is a lot of unlearning that has to happen before the good work can really begin. As I helped to build groups, I saw many friends and colleagues become less capable of listening, observing, and offering a healing presence after completing their education and licensure than when they began. There are plenty of exceptions to this, of course, but I have experienced far too many practitioners of mental health doing a poor job or even causing harm. Many agencies were involved with helping members of my family, and most failed or discouraged us. I had to find a better way.

I tried to create a team that would integrate the good practices I had experienced in business, education, international development and faith and health organizations. I found some people who were willing to experiment, and together we created groups that were focused on art, music, disk golf, or cooking—healing and learning were slipped in the back door. When the people genuinely enjoyed each other, trusted each other with their questions and struggles, and wanted to be together, they were more open to learning and growth. We often felt like we were using a Patch Adams-type approach, where enjoying the process and people were the highest priorities.

We had plenty of mess-ups, but we learned from them, and those who stayed around grew to tolerate short-term mistakes because they saw how they often led to opportunities for growth.

(*Minnie*) You are going to have to show me how this played out in Grace's story because I can see the big ideas, but don't know how to measure the results. How did you identify and break the generational chains (those *Dead Patterns* you mention) that kept people from growth?

(*Eric*) It's actually a very good start to find and name the *Dead Patterns*. Doing so shows they are not part of the person. So many of the lies that prop up dead patterns begin with the fear that a life-draining cycle or experience will last forever. Another good beginning point is to realize that the dead pattern was once built for seemingly good reasons. If they can rediscover that reason, they can reach the good in a different way. This goes back to the Three Steps Out exercise I talked about before.

As the dead patterns are identified, they can be seen as hollow repetition and rooted in confusion. Finding exceptions to the rules of the pattern can point the way out. As we saw, Grace was terrified whenever anything good happened to her because she feared it was the beginning of a potential loss. She had lost a great deal and felt she couldn't bear to lose any more. When I was able to help her laugh or unconsciously enjoy herself, she could internalize the exception of a good experience without loss. Her dead pattern weakened with this realization. This focuses her efforts to changing the dead pattern instead of hurting herself or her loved ones. Then reassurance, practice, and repetition builds the new, healthy pattern.

Petra's story also gets at the heart of your question. She often built little tastes of healthy community by putting her heart forward even when it was bleeding from when she was misunderstood as a threat. It's really a story of persistent courage.

This time, after they stand up to signal the end of this portion of the interview, I walk out with them. I hold Becka's gnarled hand as the others carry the casket out of the room. Becka being here has softened me even more; I feel like the group of us are all becoming something like friends, even though I still don't know much about the others. I find myself drawn to Minnie and the richness in her that seems born of pain. She has to be intentional about who she is and where she is going without the ease of a firm identity or place to fall back on, and it has given her movements an elegance that often comes from suffering without rigidity. Her body expresses her inner growth and resilience.

Feeling freer, I leave the room and wander the pub until the next interview. I'm not worried about the outcome, looking instead for the deeper things that drew me into writing the book in the first place.

The pub is full. Normally a place full of diverse people like this distracts me; my senses latch onto all the clues that surround them, and I try to piece together their stories. But I don't feel distracted now, and it's a relief. There is something about this long evening in the back room with this uncommon group of people that has quieted my mind.

Powerful elements circle inside me, trying to find a place to settle. This mysterious process of holding tensions that have not yet resolved has happened to me before, but it often causes me to feel uneasy, restless, tired, or detached. This time it's different.

The incomplete triquetra comes to mind, and rather than feeling like I need solve the puzzle, I instead feel like a child waiting to receive a long-anticipated present. Death (as a silly skeleton) has done the work for me by putting all I've learned and processed into proper proportion so they can come together and form a better whole.

*Perception, **perspective**, and **proportion**, then, complete the triquetra of seeing, and **integration** is the golden circle binding them together. Now, **discernment** is possible. I stop and sketch the newly completed triquetra with the ring so that I won't forget it. I love the infinite nature of it—a wholeness of mind, heart, and senses.*

*In my mind, I see this capacity **embodied** in a unique human being: it is the sum of their relationship with themselves, with others, and with the universe—their **presence** that reconciles all the darkness and light of their life into an untaintable center (like what Eden experienced). Reciprocal Dignity becomes like breathing, allowing the good to come in and out—into the core of one human and out into others.*

I am in awe. I feel tiny and vast simultaneously. We humans are so much more than short lives and small perspectives. A meta-symbol made of all the symbols of the night is forming in my mind. Maybe the task this group had given me—to integrate the symbols—is happening!

More is stirring inside me. The theatre of the evening, crafted to bring me back to myself, is a new gateway to understanding. I see the classic masks of Comedy and Tragedy summing up all human experience, melding with Lady Wisdom. I try a sketch to see a little of what this image is becoming.

I am eager to see more of the fullness of this wisdom image, but I know the last story about Petra needs to be shared before I will be free to imagine it completely. Her story affirms what is being forged inside me. Becoming her friend and sharing in her life freed the good in each of us and released it into the world.

Dear Reader,

What if the capacity to hold wisdom is a gift? How would we discern whether a person has that gift or not? A related question is this: Are people who experience mental illness or intense suffering able to discern who would be a good, wise counselor?

The answer is more likely to be "yes" if they are a part of a community experienced in combining different perceptions and perspectives. I have seen this done in organizations where many types of people really have a voice. One organization, called CHARG, has two full boards of directors, one that is made of entirely of "consumers" and another of "community members." They take the time to find full agreement among both boards on major issues, and this often opens up a third way not seen at first by either board.

One time the consumers wanted to give raises to the staff because of how excellent their care had been, but the community board were concerned it was not fiscally responsible to do so. It seemed like a deadlock, but they let the tension remain until they found a third way. Eventually they all agreed to initiate new fundraising efforts which made it fiscally possible to give the raises.

Perhaps a person who has experienced the mental health system first-hand might know a thing or two about it. Could this be honored in the same manner as a community member with experience in nonprofit finance? Yes!

Another organization I am in friendship with is called Project I See You. After a decade of mutually empowering work with women in multiple countries, the leaders discovered that they had fallen into a compassionate silence about their own roles and needs. They needed insight that would free them from a system of their own making. This system was doing a great deal of good, but blocked speaking truth in love. It required the risk of hurting one another to find a new basis.

People in transition or who don't tend to fit the existing systems can teach us a lot about what those systems are lacking. Similarly, people who are not like us can often teach us the most about ourselves. They ask questions we wouldn't know to ask.

E

VII

THE WEIGHT OF PRIMAL TRUTH

A Dream of Wise Counsel

*I feel my presence reflected in others—**more** gentle, **more** open, **more** ready*

*Do I know **more** or know now that I know less?*

I laugh with my absurd enjoyment in being.

I offer what I have and find it replenished.

I stumble and hear echoes of falls —

I try to armor myself and find my skin is too soft for such ways.

(*Eric*) *When I met Petra, she brought in two baseball cards with her sons' pictures on them. Baseball was, for them, a hard-earned success; it felt as if it was one of very few successes they could claim. She told me they were terrified of school—just driving near one would make them hide or cringe. One son wore many layers of clothing whenever he left the house. The other, Tim, refused to go to the dentist or brush his teeth, and because of this, had many dental problems. He would become violent and break things, so that anyone around him had to lock themselves in a room and wait for him to calm down. He would not eat or drink unless it fit a very narrow list of requirements and was served to him. She explained that the boys did not want to meet in an office and had resisted going to see the psychiatrist. If I wanted to meet with them, it would have to be at their house.*

As I got to know Petra, I learned her marriage was falling apart and that her school district, medical professionals, and all-male workplace (run by her husband) felt threatening, so she operated on high alert. Through our meetings together, I was able to help her see that despite so many people disagreeing with her, she usually knew what was best for her children and had the most clues about what to try next. Our conversations flowed easily because she intuited that I truly respected who she was and what she valued in life.

Petra learned that she had to stop listening to what everyone was telling her to do, calm herself, and carve out protected spaces for her and her boys to try little steps forward. She had to share how bad it had become in order to break the idea that she was the failure at the center of it all.

But before we could tackle those issues inside her, we needed to address her present problem—her boys. So we planned and enacted hundreds of small steps that eventually helped them break their social anxieties, return to school, and begin adding new capacities to their lives. They were part of the disk golf group I helped create that modeled good social skills. We taught medical professionals how to see "resistant" behaviors differently, and educators how to carefully build on successes to reduce fear.

As we worked, it became more and more clear to me that Petra was the key to it all. I recognized that my time, influence, and presence were far more limited than the mother's, so I shifted our time to focus on strengthening her, and the results came far more quickly because of this.

It wasn't easy, though, because Petra had been taught by key people in her life that she was not a good person. She confided to me that she would likely have killed herself long ago if her sons hadn't needed her. She was still sometimes tempted by suicide, and she frequently walked away from encounters with people feeling like she was "trash," not deserving to live.

In my eyes, she was a very gifted and rare woman who seemed immune to many of the problems that drag down American women. She was honest, down-to-earth, practical, warm, kind, and naturally acquired wisdom. But Petra lacked the ability to protect herself in some key ways that caused her to suffer intensely through most of her life. Her good qualities were often misinterpreted, and she believed the misinterpretations because they were so frequently reflected back to her as reality.

In one of our sessions, she told me her story to shed light on how she perceived herself.

(**Petra**) As a young person, I did well in school but struggled with people and with my feelings. I was a visual learner, which made it really hard to connect with people when I couldn't see them, like talking on the phone—"I don't even know what these people are saying," I'd say to myself. It was as if I needed to see what was going on between myself and the other person before their words made sense to me.

I improved over time with practice. I can talk on the phone now because I look up and to the right into space, imagining what the person looks like in order to sense their feelings, intentions, and in-stinctual reactions. It happens almost on an animal level. For the lon-gest time, I didn't know that other people don't see like this, or that I respond to actual intentions rather than words. People often say to me, "I didn't say that," or "You shouldn't know that." It's because I'm not responding to their fabricated presence. Animals have always been easier for me to relate to because they don't have a fake way of relat-ing; they are more pure.

Being a visual person helped me get good grades all through school because I could visualize the page, and the memory of it would stay for quite a while. I don't practice it as much now, so it's harder, but it would come back if I wanted.

I don't know what it was like for my mom and dad to be parents. They started divorcing when I was eight and finalized it when I was eleven. Dad withdrew without giving any reasons other than that mom said he was an alcoholic, but I never saw it. There was no alco-hol in our home; I never saw him drunk, and I never saw him drink alcohol. He smoked cigarettes all the time, but I never smelled alco-hol, though I know he went to AA. One good memory from third to fifth grade was that we would lie on the couch together and watch football.

My whole family wasn't really involved with me. I always did my homework alone, except for one time when I did a major project on Egypt and made a reed boat out of pussywillow reeds I picked from a nearby wetland. The boat was four feet long and actually worked. It was one of the few things my mom did with me. We soaked the reeds in the bathtub, bundled them, and made them into a boat shape with a mast and sail. Then I carried it to school on a wagon.

Mom seemed to know something was different about me, but nothing was done. I was disappointed that she didn't try to figure it out or get help. I'd cry and cry, and she would listen to me, but that was all.

Dad was mostly not there for me, and he was judgmental when I did talk to him. I told him, "I think I need help." He said, "Why would you want that?" I didn't understand why he would respond that way.

After the divorce, Mom had many boyfriends. When I was between eleven and thirteen years old, she had a boyfriend who had a motorcycle. I was scared when mom would go out and stay out late because I thought she would crash and die. On those nights I'd sleep in my sister's room.

My sister competed with me from a very early age. She got B's and C's as a student while I got straight A's, but she had girlfriends, which of course was difficult for me to have.

I couldn't figure out why I didn't fit into the social atmosphere. Boys were easier than girls; even now females often seem to hate me. It's like they want to throw up when they get to know me, and I don't know why. But guys are often problems too—they want to have me too much. Somehow, I send them a message that they should come and get me. I've always tried to be friends, but they'd try to go out with me. Even in elementary school, boys chased me around, and usually the worst boy chased me the most.

I seemed to end up with chaotic, dangerous guys, because they aggressively pursued me. I often said okay because I needed a boyfriend, but I was always scared to break up because the guy might try to do something violent.

In college I had no friends; only a boyfriend, an older guy who was not too wild. He was intellectual, a drummer, and interested in business. We were together for two or three years until I started to fall apart, then we somehow broke up. I cried every day—as soon as I left class, while I ate, all the time. I tried distracting myself by joining the marching band because when I wasn't busy, I was crying. It wasn't crying because of sadness, I was crying because I was overwhelmed. I had finally reached the point where I couldn't handle people or myself.

I went to doctors to get help, but most of them were unsympathetic and sometimes even threatening. I went to a clinic once because my legs itched so badly I wanted to cut them off. There was no rash, just uncontrollable itching. It felt like the rash was *inside*. But I received no medical help that did any good. They said, "You're showering too often," or "It's just dry skin," or "I think it's hormonal." One older male doctor said, "How about getting some psychiatric help?" but what I heard him really saying was, "Either shut up or go to the psychiatrist."

I went to a therapist and told him that if I were a man, I probably would be more violent: "I want to kill people. I'm out of control of myself." I could understand people like that on TV or in books. The therapist said I could be a serial killer, and we acknowledged that was scary. I didn't really want to do that, but I was scared of myself.

My mom thought my crying had to do with my parents' divorce, so she sent me to see a counselor to deal with it. She was a Buddhist counselor, and I cried so much that she immediately sent me to a psychiatrist who diagnosed me with anxiety and depression. I decided to take it seriously, so I went to two therapy meetings and one psychiatric group per week. I took an anti-depressant and was shocked at how much better I felt. I was angry no one told me about this earlier! The treatment also helped my social anxiety. Despite everything, I still got good grades and graduated from college summa cum laude.

After graduation I applied for a job training dogs and moved there to work. I wasn't functioning well and felt stressed out by my co-workers. The men there came from training military dogs, so they treated me in a military manner and I couldn't handle how harsh they were. There was a lot of hazing and I was made fun of, felt unsupported, and had a lot of pressure put on me. Everyone always told me to do what I was passionate about, which was working with animals, but this world did not seem to fit me.

I had a couple of more serious boyfriends during this time. I was always committed when I dated someone, as if I were married. Sex happened, but it wasn't connected to feeling married; rather I was drawn to the familiarity of intense attraction.

After about a year, I went to work at a gift shop in a wild animal park. I hated it. It was torture to have so many interesting animals nearby and to have to do shallow retail. I was still falling apart, so I quit after just under a year and moved back home. I didn't work for two years and began to shut down. I had a dog, went hiking, and did intensive therapy. It was so hard to have gotten straight A's in school but to be so unsuccessful and directionless in life.

I finally got a job at a vet clinic. The vet was a man who liked me for all the wrong reasons, but I just wanted the job. The office manager was a woman and she fired me after six months because she thought I was causing problems with the vet.

I've learned that people who want to help me do it for the wrong reasons, but it's all I have. I stopped hoping for friends and this lasted even into my forties.

I think things get stuck at what you learn at a young age. My family didn't help me learn how to make friends. I kept running into people who are like my sister or turbulent girlfriends. People will take me if I sell myself to them, but I have to be interested in what they are interested in: "You have to think what I think and do what I do, or you're out." I guess I do have a limit, though. My sister joined a cult and she completely belongs to them now. I'm not willing to sell myself like that. But I have sold myself hundreds of times to men, not with money but with my identity. To get into their club, I have to say, "Yes, I will do your bidding." But I will not sell myself to women.

When I met Mitch, he seemed to have all the things that I didn't. He could get people to love him easily and could get them to do things for him. He wasn't good at details, but I was great at that. I could stand behind him and feel somewhat protected while he charmed everyone. We got married and were a good business team. He used me and my money to do things that he wanted and buy fancy things that made him look good, while I covered for all his weaknesses. We built a successful business, but when we had children and the economy went down, the pressure started to build again. I came to see that everything revolved around him, and that if our work team and I didn't perform the way he wanted, we were useless to him. He wanted to be adored, and the men who worked with him did that, but after a while I didn't. He knew something was wrong and tried to make me into a sex-focused person to make up for it. That's when I realized he was addicted to all kinds of things that gave him little rushes of pride, and if I wasn't going to be one of those things then he would try to emotionally manipulate me. He didn't like that our kids weren't normal and eventually he detached from us. I felt like trash almost every day. No one was helping me with our boys, and everyone seemed to blame me. Mitch told me in a million ways that I was useless and a failure, and the men in the company picked up on that and told me similar things through their actions.

I finally divorced Mitch because I felt like I was dead inside and that he was married to other people. He quickly found a rich, sexy woman, married her, and started using her and her family to live the high life he couldn't have with me and my kids. It was crushing. I felt like I was nothing and that no one would ever love or understand me again. It was like all my feelings and intuitions were magnified and pointed toward being lost and worthless.

I think my mom suffered like this too. It probably hurt her to see it happening to me. She wanted to help but didn't know how to help herself, much less me. We are alike in that she sensed and saw too much, and it overwhelmed her. She got into New Age beliefs because they helped normalize and explain her differences.

Once when I visited my mom after she had been diagnosed with cancer, I asked you, Eric, to come with me because she fell on the bathroom floor and I needed help getting her up. She was so anxious that we spent some time with her after we got her to her bed. After she calmed down, she just laid there like she was in a fog. She was present, but not fully. We went down the hall to talk, but she called me back saying she wanted to talk with you.

I was surprised because I hadn't talked with her mother very much and she wanted me to come visit her alone. At her bedside, she reached out her hand and I held it for a little while. She looked up at the ceiling, and the fog seemed to lift. She looked directly into my eyes and gripped my hand tightly, saying in a clear, direct voice, "You are going to break the chains that have shackled our family for generations." I didn't know what to say, but I felt as if a massive amount of energy was pouring out of her into my chest. Tears filled my eyes, and I held her hand in silence. After about a minute, she let go and laid back in bed. The fog seemed to cover her up again and her breathing became raspier.

I still don't fully understand what happened that day, but I've had many encounters with people since then which are ultimately revealed to be about "chains of generations." This encounter gave me a lens to see those experiences that I didn't have before.

As time passed, my conversations with Petra helped her shift her thinking and emotions. She began to see them as finely tuned instruments that she could learn to control. They weren't gateways to death and chaos, but they did take in things that she had to learn to tune out or understand differently than "I must be trash." Sometimes it was clear how she changed as she latched

onto a new understanding and found ways to repeat it over and over to her-
self until she deeply absorbed it. Sometimes she would find music that would
soothe her and listen to it with tea to nurture herself. At times, I didn't under-
stand how she was changing, and I would ask about it.

I am learning to teach myself that hard things always pass, so I don't
have to gear up as much when I sense them coming. I tell myself,
"This is not permanent. There is a solution. You can change it. It
seems like this will be forever, but it's not."

In the past, if someone had told me that I could think differently,
I would have said they were crazy. But now I've learned it is possible
after all! When I get overwhelmed or feel like I'm trash, I remind myself that these thoughts will be there, but I don't have to feed them.
It's like an addiction—I have to see what it is without denying it, and
then stop feeding it. I have to assume it will come back throughout
my life, at any time, and yet not be afraid of it. I have to not be surprised when those thoughts come or feel guilty when I stumble. I
need to expect them to return and not be derailed. I used to hold
onto those dark things because they were familiar, comfortable. But I
don't need to anymore.

How did you break from the familiar to find something better?

I had to use some of the parenting methods I learned for my boys on myself. A few years ago, I had the choice between a part-time job that wasn't a good fit for me and a full-time job that was. I had believed for a long time that I couldn't work anymore because of my social fears. I was used to zero doors being open, but here were two that had opened without much effort—one was easier, and one was harder. I went for the harder job, but without expectation. I knew it was the door for me because it was the one that would allow me to grow into a better person. I was deathly afraid during every step of applying, starting, and getting used to my job. But I did it.

Sometimes I had to do something extreme, like getting a divorce, pulling out of school, quitting the family company, or becoming a Christian when my husband didn't like any of it. Sometimes it felt like the godly part of me wanted me to grow. Once I realized I'm not completely in control, that there's something or someone else who has my best interest in mind, I could rest a little. I could take little risks and try new things, which became more natural.

Was the change lasting?

Sometimes the old beasts revisit, but it doesn't feel constant like in the old days, and the intensity is much less and lasts for a shorter time. When I get triggered, like when my sister implies I'm not good enough at something, I see it more clearly now and can step back instead of jumping into it. I am more detached instead of identifying with the criticism. Depression and grief come in waves, but I know how to detach from the thoughts and feelings by reminding myself that these things are not me. I'm not removed from them, but I am better at dealing with them.

Petra is in a long-term relationship now, and her boys are doing much better. She is doing well in a full-time job and she understands how to use her strengths to help other people. I am so impressed by her perseverance and hard work to get to where she is today.

She called me recently to say, "Eric, I'm learning to be shallow! I can hide myself behind 'nothing' words and 'not caring' energy. It works really well! Women aren't as scared, and men aren't trying to possess me so much!" I was happy to hear her getting the protection she needed, but sad that our culture would require that of her. "Don't use any of that stuff on me, Petra!" I said. "I like you as you are."

Another day she called and said, "I'm going to complete a master's program while working full time. I never thought I could do that. My social life is so full, it now feels like too much. I could never have imagined that. My children are doing well! We are going to the theatre, I am training horses, and my life is so full I can't tell you about it all!" A grin stuck to my face for quite a while after hanging up from that phone call. She later texted, "Thank you for being the right guy, at the right place, at the right time to fit with us when we needed it."

As time went on, our conversations became less frequent and they tended to tackle increasingly complex relational issues. Petra became more and more comfortable in her own skin, aware of how to use her strengths, and capable of navigating the stress that came when she was overwhelmed or sensed hostile intent. She could now handle what she used to call "too much truth." I knew she had reached a new pinnacle when, for the first time, I lavished praise on her for her achievements and she was able to simply receive it. No discomfort, shifting, or giggling; just awareness of having been given a challenging gift which she could now use for good.

The Weight of Primal Truth—Analysis

Summary

A woman with uncommon strengths is misinterpreted and exploited by people who see her as an easy target or a threat. She can sense intention, cannot depart from truth, and does not understand the normal underlying threats and falsities of the people around her. She is consumed by weeping and the belief that she is trash.

The Trap

"Being very aware (high sensory reception) is often overwhelming for me. I relate more with animals than people. I have an open heart and have no protection, so people misunderstand and hurt me. I often feel like everyone is against me, that I am only used and never loved. I enter a mental death spiral that leaves me near suicide and unable to function."

The Way Out

Never Tame an Eagle

- Forcing "normal" leads to suffering.

- Uncommon strengths may need to be "wild" before they are understood.

- Identifying and practicing being a bearer of uncommon strengths is needed.

A Firefly Looks Like A Fly On Fire

- Uncommon strengths can be perceived as weaknesses.

- A good quality can be made harmful in the name of getting along.

- Feeling overwhelmed can seem like a problem with who I am (too sensitive) instead of a problem with input processing (discernment).

★

The end is looming. It's clear on all of our faces. I'm struck to see that all the interviewers are feeling what I am. We don't want it to end. My mind is full of questions. My heart is full of potential. We sit quietly together, and somehow the silence is not awkward. There are small exchanges of warmth that remind me of trying to connect with people who do not speak English. It's as if the limits placed on our communication cause a gentle gaze, a soft word, a slow smile to have more connective weight. I stand with these people and see that they are offering me a level of respect that is foreign to me.

This respect is not effusive affirmation; it's not about glory. Somehow, we are revering each other and what we have been given without smoothing over our weaknesses. This gives me a new sense of reciprocal dignity that I had not seen before. Sometimes we need to be limited in order to find something better than what we currently see.

The type of attunement which allows my wife and me to communicate through tiny gestures and facial expressions seems to have happened here as well. I can tell they are ready to begin and there is nothing to be said before this is done. In my new sense of freedom, I decide to start the interview. My answers feel more direct and more comfortable as I give them. Inside I say thank you to my dear Becka, big old Bunsen, intense little Ebony, elegant Minnie, and compassionate Cross. Thank you too to the old woman behind the scenes who has somehow pulled us together and helped draw out more than we ever could have planned.

(Eric) Petra taught me how invisible pressures in our culture try to homogenize us. People who are different tend to feel these pressures more than those who are accepted, because they are pressured to change themselves to fit in.

Petra may be genetically wired to be more honest and live in more integrity than the vast majority of people I know. We might call this good, but being this type of person automatically forces others to experience the contrast in themselves—the lies they embrace and the manipulative games they play. Someone like Petra, then, becomes the enemy, and she has been trained to believe that this is true.

Often our work together has been to see and utilize her gifts so that she cannot deny them any longer. This is not easy. When she was almost done with her master's degree, someone questioned whether it was from a reputable school, and she was ready to agree with them that her degree was not good enough. When she started setting boundaries against the disrespect she was willing to receive, she was frequently called selfish. Often the purity or goodness of one person can provoke the anger and frustration of another. There are ways in which I am also more innocent than your average American man in his forties. I have found that this quality helps me as a counselor, and

I don't want to lose it even though it caused me a great deal of pain when I was younger. This innocence protects and softens me in ways that my experience and "savvy" do not.

(*Ebony*) I don't understand what you mean by *a Fly on Fire* versus a *Firefly*. Are you saying that less common strengths can seem bad because people don't understand their use?

(*Eric*) How would a firefly appear to you if you had no idea what one was? In ancient civilizations, light and fire were often seen as essentially the same. Wouldn't such a person name a glowing insect a "fire" fly instead of a glowing fly? Might they imagine the fly to be hot or tortured with constant inner flames?

I spent much of my early life believing that gifts I had were not masculine or not even good. I often compromised elements of myself in order to be accepted. I lost opportunities in theatre because I was too ashamed of being a teenage boy who liked to sing.

Sometimes uncommon strengths are more subtle. If a person imagines more vividly when others do not, they might be called unfocused, lazy, or impractical. If a person perceives emotional or relational dynamics but doesn't know how to separate themselves from their perceptions, they are likely to be seen as stressed, shut down, or wanting to escape. Being *overwhelmed* can be seen externally as an inability to cope. Alternatively, it could reveal toxicity in the social environment that others just take for granted because it affects them less.

(*Minnie*) How can we honor these uncommon gifts so that they flourish, instead of causing a person to suffer?

(*Eric*) It's best if we can begin early. One of my favorite quotes re-garding this topic is by William Inge, who wrote, "The proper time to influence the character of a child is about a hundred years before he is born." We not only need to recognize and assist in the training of uncommon strengths, but we also need to create legacies within communities of adults to learn how to honor emerging rare strengths. We also need to embrace Eden's lesson of *Good Appetite, Good Human.* It takes time to get comfortable with our own good and the good in others.

Becka suddenly gets a strange look on her face: very loving, and a little impish.

(*Becka*) Thank you for letting me rest in your gaze and in your words, Eric.

(*Eric*) Um, wow, Becka. Thanks.

(*Becka*) Mmm-hmm. Developing an appetite to receive the good . . . I'm not flattering you. I am stating the truth.

(*Eric*) I do need to practice what I preach. It's not easy. I don't know if I can accept such goodness—it seems like too much.

(*Becka*) How would a person who found some freedom while meet-ing with you describe you?

(*Eric*) Okay, now you're just picking on me. I'm uncomfortable with that question because I don't want the focus on me, and you know that.

(*Becka*) If you want to model receiving love and respect, because that's what you want us to do, you have to get past that.

(Eric) Why do I like you again?

(Becka) Because I am so sweet and kind. Now answer the question!

(Eric) Okay. Okay . . . hmm. One of the ladies in these stories approached me after overcoming a great deal of her own pain and said she wanted to speak into my life. Her eyes were fiery and her heart soft, and I knew I had no choice in the matter. I sat down, and she pulled out a piece of paper with some prepared words and poured them into me. I have it here with me because it encourages me on days when I doubt myself. Here is what she said,

> You are a strong man.
> You walk on the edges of what is possible,
> You have been given a gift,
> You carry a light and are luminous,
> You bring healing power through safe understanding,
> In being known, we are freed.

Why did she say this? Because I walked with her through hard things. I walked in the mud with her, and because of that I saw things in her that no one else saw. Together we found ways for her hidden strengths to come out and become natural.

We can all learn to do such things, but first they must be seen as treasures worthy of pursuit. It is important to note that I could not have done this unless she chose to let me into her world. She had to decide if my life, experiences, choices, and beliefs had made me a person worth trusting with her highly protected, wounded self.

This woman focused on my strengths, but my weaknesses could also be seen as part of what happened. Not fitting in and having long-term suffering in my family gives me a compassion I wouldn't have had without many days and nights of parenting failure, sorrow from being misunderstood, exhaustion, and loneliness from challenges that, in the long run, were excellent training for understanding the suffering of others.

(*Becka*) You do have a thirst for wisdom. What have you found in doing your work that fulfills you?

(*Eric*) I often feel like I need a book to answer each of your questions, Becka. Remembering how I prepared for this book strikes me as important. I spoke to numerous people about wisdom and how we can receive it. I began to see that Wisdom was more plentiful than it seemed to me initially. My impression was that few people intentionally valued Her anymore. But developing a sense of abundance changed my focus from one of walking in a desert to one of gathering what was spread out.

A professor friend told me of three classic gateways to wisdom:

- The often-natural intuition of women—because being immersed in life reveals its intricacies. It is the wisdom of the powerfully *intimate inside*.

- The often-natural male detachment—which allows an outside perspective of things and is vital to understanding. It is a wisdom of the bold and *vast outside*.

- The last gateway is the most rare—male-cultivated intuition (sometimes called gut reaction) or female-cultivated detachment (freedom from overwhelming immersion or perception) in which the internal and external perspectives are integrated. This gateway leads to the most truth, because it gives lived experiences the context of the cosmos in correct proportion to the present.

Maybe this is why I needed the help of these women to tell my story more fully. We needed each other's perspectives as well as our own perception of what was happening while working together.

If we understand what wisdom is and where we might find it, perhaps we won't as easily fall into isolation, polarization, or mental illness. It's clear that stress and isolation exacerbate the inner knots of the mind and body.

(*Cross*) I want to be a wise healer. What can I do to prepare myself?

(*Eric*) A therapist friend who accomplishes a great deal in a psychiatric hospital says, "We must develop the gravity to have strength of character and humanity so the chaotic and disturbing does not shake our core. We must be salty to cause others to thirst for that which, by its nature, is healing and strengthening."

How is this done? Another friend described it as learning to walk on the thresholds of change while seeking experiences that strengthen and give peace. For me, that began with not having a stable career, not having the easy connection that comes with being like most men, and later learning to enjoy people who are on the fringe with me. This built up a tolerance to "dying" to things that really do not matter, which allows energy to be freed for what does.

(*Bunsen*) What is the risk of helping people this way?

(*Eric*) One of my recurring nightmares involves the risks of pride and short-term success. In it, I am only helping people for my own sake or in ways that only equip them to be good consumers—not truly better people. Another risk is that reciprocal dignity is powerful and intimate. The power and intimacy can be poorly handled, and the dignity lost. Growing in integrity of self requires time investments into relationships that reveal early signs of these hazards.

I have been given some specific kinds of suffering that have been key to understanding how to handle these risks. I have felt trapped, and this has shown me the value and sweetness of freedom. I have felt unseen, which has shown me the glory of being intimately known. I have been overwhelmed, and so cherish peace. I do not wish these conditions on anyone, but it is harder to fear them when one sees their potential.

So many human pains are repeated because the wisdom woven into the experience is not learned or passed on. There are important human treasures that cannot be given as information.

What we are doing together with these stories is creating what is beyond the words themselves—an experience with the real people who are now sharing what they have learned to help others. It is in coming alongside one another—walking together—that wisdom is often found.

A time of quiet comes. It's not that we have run out of questions or answers, but we are pausing to appreciate the fact that this group has become closer. We have shared so little time, but in a surprising way, so much. I want them to understand the fragile hope I have.

(Eric) You have all helped me so much with my struggle to express how to pursue wisdom through reciprocal dignity. I'm very thankful. I want to tell you about an experience that reminds me this road is worth walking.

A tiny, blonde-haired girl heard the reverent tones in the voices of her parents as they talked about an upcoming counseling appointment, as they said, "Mommy and Daddy are getting help so that our family will be stronger." Because they couldn't get a babysitter, she was going to go with them. This little girl was so excited about going to this mysterious place called "counseling" that she exhausted herself and fell asleep during the first meeting. For the next meeting, she was determined to stay awake and played little games with herself to remain alert. When she arrived at the office, she was the first one in the door and thrust herself into the room with a look of complete openness and readiness. It was as if, with her little chin, bold eyes, and squared shoulders, she said, "Counsel me! I am ready for anything!"

It's a picture of what I would love counseling to become.

Each of you drew some important things out of me and each other in these discussions. Here are a few that are still humming in my mind.

Who doesn't need wise counsel? Why does counseling need to be limited to a medical model that says you must have an illness or something wrong with you in order to get it? Even clear psychiatric disorders must be addressed by a combination of actions that not only get at the physiological (the chemistry of the brain) but also a person's beliefs, perceptions, and understandings. The scientific study of mental illness, the brain, and the body are very important, but good counsel requires more than this information.

Effective healers must be humble enough to listen well and develop a readiness to receive and learn. The belief that you have all, or even most, of the answers is actually a barrier. A lack of curiosity or humility was the first indication that a health professional would likely be of little help when my wife and I tried to get help for our family.

In preparing to see, effective healers cultivate curiosity, courage, and interest that allow them to walk alongside people peacefully even when the circumstances may not be. They often work very hard and are persistent and enduring, but ultimately they are not driven by a need for common rewards. They accept people where they are because they know there are important realities that brought them there. They allow themselves to grow from encounters because they have done the work to be ready.

Let us gain from the science of humanity without assuming it is the sole voice. Let us listen to the data of humanity without assuming it stands unaffected by that which cannot be measured. Let us not forget that life is constantly in motion, in change, and in becoming. Within every person are elements that can move toward balance. When there is an imbalance, we are attempting to help a body and mind out of a position in which its own capacities are moving in declining (depressing), ambivalent, conflicting, or escalating (anxious) directions. These movements, like all human behavior, always have a reason, a basis, and do not come ex nihilo. When this basis is found, the triggers, the responses, the perceptions, and the exertions make sense, and missing pieces can be found to bring the person back to balance and peace. It may be a complex story, but chaos does not reign inside the human.

(*Bunsen*) Thank you, Eric. Those are good reflections. It is time for this to end now. A few of us will stay and answer some questions, but I want you to know that we appreciate what you are doing and we are your friends in this effort.

I want to find a way to go deeper but also not waste my chance for questions. So I blurt out, "Do you all work for Psyche?"

(*Minnie*) Most of us do not. We were all invited to come here just as you were. We are all interested in wisdom and were asked to partic-ipate in this experiment. The goal was to gather wisdom from your experiences and fit them into some sort of larger compilation. None of us has seen the larger chronicle, but the eldress has. We are all go-ing back to our normal lives with the hope that we will be called again. This has been an amazing experience. Thank you.

(*Eric*) Wait. Are you saying that you all are as new to this as I am?

(*Cross*) Some of us had been interviewed like you, and some were just invited to be interviewers. Our invitations said, "*Psyche* recogniz-es you for your excellent work in your field. We would like to invite you to a discussion, which we believe you will find fruitful. Please come to our informal location listed below." When we arrived, we were given some standards to follow, like not giving our names, and that was about it. But the questions came from us reading your stories and wanting to understand them.

(*Eric*) Why are you so careful about what you say and don't say? I feel like everything is so mysterious.

(*Minnie*) Out of respect for the good work you have already done, we have chosen to keep some distance from you. We want to encourage you. We want to show you that you are not alone and that your work is worth doing. However, we have too often accidentally influenced efforts like yours in ways that harmed their early growth. Out of respect for you, we are staying in the background for now. Consider us your friends. Don't think of us as some kind of secretive group that creates mystery in order to trick people into perpetuating some agenda. We have real concerns that this period in human history is experiencing a poverty of wisdom. Its skills in forming communities capable of living expressions of wisdom are weak. We work to change that, and you do as well. Please be patient in our relationship; your patience will prove to be worthwhile. Thank you for sharing your heart and mind with us today.

The group begins to disperse, but I have to sit down. This last exchange breaks something loose inside me and then surprisingly gives me a sense of solidity. The dignity Minnie is referring to seems to require trusting in something larger than our individuality. The reciprocity needs to be intentional, but not orchestrated. It as if we have all been given different kinds of jewels and have been tasked with putting them to good use. This begins with honoring what we had been given and sharing it wisely, without force and without fear, but instead with hopeful connection. It's as if I have broken away from some sort of isolation and brought into some larger good.

Perhaps this frees my mind, because the symbols come into my imagination again and come together in a new, more complete way. This time I am seeing a mask that makes me feel like I am witnessing the depth and richness I hear in the old woman's voice, but now in a younger form. My first impression is that she is vibrant like I might imagine a truly noble, royal woman to be. She is formed by the comedy mask with a triquetra over her eyes and the golden circle for an integration crown. I feel as if she sees more than regular humans; her gaze is penetrating, but joyfully so. Looking at the triquetra and remembering the previous symbol integration, I call it three-sighted. A sun surrounds her face; the flames of its brightness blend with her flowing hair. This strange woman is unobtainable; she is a mask we all can wear for a time to see more, to embody more, and to laugh at darkness, but then we have to take the mask off and live. She resides in the fabric of the universe, throughout all of time, in all living beings, and cannot be held completely by any of them. I don't fully understand this vision. It disconcerts me to feel as if I am holding something important, but it isn't really mine—I don't know what to do with it.

The symbols have come together but I don't understand what they have become. Why a mask? I don't want to hide or pretend. I don't want to step into fantasy. This is my life. This book is important to me… It hits me. This

is why the coffin comedy came earlier... I was holding onto what was happening too tightly. I don't want to do that again. I try to let go even more.

Maybe I can't control what is happening to me. Is it my intuition or the muse of imagination or the old woman? I don't know. As I release my inner struggle, my breathing deepens, my mind slows, and my being seems to lighten again. I won't reject this integration of symbols so fast. I will see what can be learned. I try to bring back curiosity.

What would I do if I were a little kid? I would want to try it on! I would want to try being this strange Lady Wisdom—even if I didn't understand her—even if she is a woman and I am not—even if I didn't know what would happen.

As I imagine putting on the mask, I receive again what the six women have given me:

THE GIFT OF RECEPTIVITY
They could have blocked, run, refused—protected—instead they shared their vulnerability and offered connection. In this gift we both receive.

THE GIFT OF RESONANCE
Trust opened the way to connection, and shared elements were found, acknowledged, explored, and used for the greater good. In this gift we both grow in understanding.

THE GIFT OF RESPECT
"I carry you in the back of my mind for when I need advice or encouragement." In this gift we both are honored.

Each unique woman drew out unique aspects of me. I had to solidify and clarify things that were nebulous inside me for the sake of caring for and liberating another—their specific needs created a frame for me to paint within in order to discover colors within myself that had not yet been called out.

Because of these reciprocal gifts, they are now connected to me—a part of me—like daughters, sisters, and friends because of the sharing of time, hearts, minds, and hope.

By putting on the mask, I see myself. I see through the eyes of these women and know myself better. I'm seen and it is changing me.

I want to tell the interviewers what is happening inside me, but the group is breaking up.

The only ones left in the room are Becka, Bunsen, and Ebony. I have so many questions. I want to find out what will happen next! It doesn't seem right to ask that. Something about the reverence of this moment makes me want to stay quiet.

As we turn the lights down and the shadows grow, the four of us stand in a slipshod circle and receive the final moments. There are some tears. I wonder if this will be Becka's last journey, as coming to the end allows her to show the full weight of her pain. I can't dwell on that concern right now.

There are some laughs. We remember our tricks, fears, and silly pride. The closing words and embraces last longer than they usually would for people who have known each other for only a day. Some beginnings begin. Some endings loom. Life is among us in its many forms and with its many faces. We all seem to feel what Minnie had reached out for: a unity and foundational connection we did not control, but could, at this time, savor. The interviewers walk away, and I don't see where they go because Becka draws near. As she passes, she presses a small piece of paper into my hand. "This is from my friend who you heard but have not seen." It has only two words:

Keep going.

I still have this scrap of paper, and these words soothe me and grant me a contentment that lasts to this day.

Dear Reader,

Are you disturbed by the thought of wearing the mask of a three-sighted woman? Such a response might fit a threshold between the known and the unknown. For who among us can expand or elevate without the fearful beauty of small disturbances or deaths? When I put on the mask, I see differently, I feel differently, and I am different. For a time, the three-sighted woman and I are one. We do not fully merge, but join and share; when I take the mask off, my walk with Lady Wisdom is not over, for she is not the mask. I need to face my disturbance at the edge of what I am and what I am becoming in order to step into a new level of relationship with her. I need a humorous casket to wake up and draw closer to my new nameless friends. I may need a mask to find what I did not know to look for.

It is common to associate a mask with falsehood or pretending to be something you are not. Good acting takes something real in the actor and connects it truthfully to the person they are temporarily being. Finding wisdom is better than "fake it till you make it." It is true becoming. It begins with finding that hunger, thirst, seed, or hope that is already there for us to honestly build upon. Many ancient traditions do this as they put on an animal identity, the mind of Christ, the cloak of righteousness, the frame of enlightenment—knowing they do not fully embody what they are putting on, but rather embracing something in it.

Once, as an actor, I had the privilege and pain of playing the role of Otto Frank, the father of Anne Frank. As I rehearsed and later put on the "Otto mask" to become him for performances, it was not sufficient to pretend or copy. For the power of his life to come out of me, I had to find and express that which was in me which was also in him. When that was accomplished, I and the audience members felt the difference. Our joys and sorrows mingled, and what came forth was something neither of us could have made on our own. These Otto/Eric moments allowed a dead man to bring new life out of me. It is another expression of reciprocal dignity—to help us find what can only be found in a relationship. This kind of relationship can disturb or even destroy that which cannot bear the heat of new life.

Æ

What I wear on and off stage is my mask. You see, a mask doesn't hide you, it exposes you.
—*Nuno Roque*

A Dream of Wise Counsel

Movements around me come in and come out with life on top of life
A new symphony surrounds but my young ears only catch short bursts
Each sequence is so rich and opens an ache
I long and for a time am held in awe

I seek her still.
I cannot make her music come.
I seek her as one in love.

Blessed is the one who finds wisdom,
and the one who gets understanding,
for the gain from her is better than gain from silver
and her profit better than gold.
She is more precious than jewels,
and nothing you desire can compare with her.
—King Solomon's Proverbs (3:13-15)

Wisdom is a gateway to reciprocal dignity and reciprocal dignity is a gateway to wisdom.

AUTHOR'S NOTE

The women in these stories are real. In order to tell their stories in a way that protects them and helps the stories intermingle, some fantasy and obscuring elements have been added. The pub interview scenes are a composite of actual situations and people, but the events did not happen as portrayed. Some identifying details have also been changed, but with the intention of staying as close to the truth as possible. The limited amount of fiction is a shield for me—in you not knowing fully what is real and what is not, I can say riskier things.

Psyche does not exist—yet.

Acknowledgments

In order to even imagine seeking wisdom, I had to be unlocked in heart and mind in ways that only a rare woman like my bride could, did, and continues to do. Her intuition of the emotional landscape and dangerous honesty have inoculated me from many inner sicknesses which have threatened to pierce my skin.

I have gratitude for my parents as providers of abundant nurture and barriers of protection from generational and local harm. Their shelter grants me the peace to write this work.

I have gratitude for the six women who generously shared their depths with me and all who read this. I care about you all deeply and hope your stories teach and liberate for many years to come. The time and effort we spent together on this work will warmly illuminate me for the rest of my life.

I have gratitude for the colleagues and friends who read various forms of this book as it was taking shape and whose corrections and ideas now live inside it; for Caleb Seeing for your developmental bind breaking and pruning and Ferris Fynboh for your fine refining; Angie Johnston, for co-creating the concept of reciprocal dignity, you managed to pack about fifty years of friendship into four; for Kim Jahn and your sharp, patient eye and great encouragement—your quests for purity encourage me; Jeremy Strand, for your insightful suggestions and patient readings. This book is better for the touches of your mind and heart.

Thank you to my friendly focus group readers who made this work better and kept me going: Brian Boisen, David Burgess, Rebecca Duncan, Steve Huff, Nena Kuhr, Øystein Levinsen, Charles and Leslie Moore, Josh Renfro, Christine Soto, and Jayne Spear.

Thank you to CHARG, Project I See You, Network Coffee House, the Bruderhof, and HomeBoy Industries for living out these ideas and practices – you inspire me.

APPENDIX A

The Way Out
Co-discovered Wisdom of Liberation

Know Thy Other
- Don't disrupt people without seeing how they fit into their world (perception).

- People have good reasons for the patterns they create (even if they contain destructive elements).

Home Dirt, Healthy Plant
- Help people where they are, with what they have.

- A good *fit* is one of the most important elements of true help.

Four Eyes First
- Respectfully uniting what the helper and sufferer see—this gives access to liberating material (perspective building).

- Sharing insights is a higher priority than a diagnosis or "answer."

Feet Build Trust

- Walk together before trying to change someone's path.

- Everyone has momentum—understand it and move with it.

A Dark Pond Still Holds Water

- Climbing out of darkness might require standing on shadows.

- Seemingly bad outcomes can contain hidden good.

Good Appetite, Good Human

- Regularly receiving good takes experience and practice.

- Giving more good requires receiving more good.

Not Given, Not Had

- The effects of neglect are often hard to see from the inside or outside.

- Missing skills and inexperience (experience poverty) require building on existing, related skills and experiences in order to enter the unknown.

- If you don't know what you don't know, and you can't see what you can't see, empathy and real understanding of the current state of things can lead to awareness of what is unknown and unseen.

Be a Bridge

- The counselor may need to be an exemplar, a

demonstrator, a real human to practice being with and re-lating to, in order to find the way forward.

- You can't go off the tracks without something good to get you there. Weaknesses and failures are often linked to unseen strengths which keep them going.

- An atrophied strength requires safe initial use during the "shaky first steps" to acquire the confidence for new hope, new trust, new understanding, and new accomplishments.

Reverse the Void

- Deeply held false beliefs can be like an illusory machine driving a person.

- When a fundamental void drives a person, it, and not the symptoms, must be found and dealt with.

- Whenever a person is diminished, drained, or anxious, look for twisted strengths, ambivalence, or unbalanced patterns—their resolution releases energy for other uses.

Dig For True Self, Not Dead Patterns

- Dead patterns are built on good intentions, which are connected to what the true self cares about.

- Hollow repetition and persistent confusion are traps, not true choices.

- Dead patterns are not a person's true self and can be changed, though doing so may feel like dying.

Never Tame an Eagle

- Forcing "normal" leads to suffering.

- Uncommon strengths may need to be "wild" before they are understood.

- Identifying and practicing being a bearer of uncommon strengths is needed.

A Firefly Looks Like a Fly on Fire

- Uncommon strengths can be perceived as weaknesses.

- A good quality can be made harmful in the name of getting along.

- Feeling overwhelmed can seem like a problem with who I am (too sensitive) instead of a problem with input processing (discernment).

APPENDIX B

THREE STEPS OUT

Reflection

- All emotions occur because of caring about something.

- You value what you care about.

- Recognizing what you value is critical to finding peace in challenging situations.

The Steps

1) Name the emotion—be specific.

From: *"People drive me crazy—they don't get me."*

To: ***I'm afraid of being misunderstood and hurt by people.***

This step slows the "echo effect" that comes from being afraid of being afraid, or being depressed about being depressed. If we are afraid of being afraid, the fear grows—if we see more clearly what we are afraid of, it shrinks a little. This step also cools the overgeneralization that happens when our brain tells us that what is in front of us now is like what has hurt us in the past. Our brains narrow our focus and seeks similar threats to past experience. We have to retrain our brains to think in specifics in order to lower our guard to a level that fits current reality.

2) Find the good behind the emotion.

"I want to be understood so I can have good relationships."

Every emotion has good within it. There is no such thing as a bad emotion. We can appreciate and use our emotions productively if we pause to find the good behind what may feel like a "bad" emotion. If we understand emotions as messengers and know that they will go away when we've received the message, we can separate ourselves from them rather than identifying with them. "No one wants to be around me because I am such an emotional mess" can become, "I need to hear what my emotions are telling me so that they don't stay around so long." Even when a whole body system is thrown off in the form of clinical depression or bipolar swings, this approach in addition to mind/body care (diet, supplements, medication, etc.) can help bring balance. Because emotions are always connected to something we care about, this can also focus the emotional energy toward the positive.

3) Take one small step into the good.

"I'm going to choose a person I want to be closer to and share one new thing with them."

Patterned, repeated behavior (or practices) toward what is good for us (or what we truly want) is the key to mental and emotional health. If we regularly step into the good that the emotion springs from, we get to act upon its core message. This allows us to see the value of our full perceptive and capability. It also trains us to receive what we sense instead of acting solely in protective, rapid reaction mode. This is a time where relational poverty is common, and this state keeps many of us in a mental mode that was meant for dangerous, no-time-to-think situations. We need each other to practice reducing small threats into the seeds of learning.

APPENDIX C

A DREAM OF WISE COUNSEL

I see the valleys and valleys filled with bondage;
They converse and confirm — so many empty nods and smiles;
They swim in lethargic waters — rippling in one ongoing, pulsing
*   pattern —*
They do not travel, only move.

I reach into the hidden, the dark, the afraid — rage greets me — pain
*   screams,*
I know them and do not waver.
Voices echo in pale, sweaty circles with no tone — they blend — they hide in
*   thought,*
I reveal them and their cowardice.
They run to softer places and begin their death spirals once again.

I walk among them.
The words we share cause wax to flow unseen from ear to pool;
A bit of awareness comes holding fear's hand,
"All is being undone! You are not safe! You are not in control! Run!"

So much rests on these moments of expansive trust or shriveling safety.

A shaking step, a fountain of tears, exhaustion, mortification,

A death of the built me –

Walls break, systems crumble – what was alive is alive again but so small,
*   so fragile.*

Is this really better than what was? Can I be a slave again?

New power – where does it go? It cannot be contained – I will not be
*   contained*

Shall I hurt, shall I please, shall I go a new way and leave all
*   behind?*

I break away and find solid ground,

I look back and find I have more than I believed possible.

*I feel my presence reflected in others—**more** gentle, **more** open, **more** ready*

*Do I know **more** or know now that I know less?*

I laugh with my absurd enjoyment in being.

I offer what I have and find it replenished.

I stumble and hear echoes of falls —

I try to armor myself and find my skin is too soft for such ways.

Movements around me come in and come out with life on top of life

A new symphony surrounds but my young ears only catch short
*   bursts*

Each sequence is so rich and opens an ache

I long and for a time am held in awe

I seek her still.

I cannot make her music come.

I seek her as one in love.

APPENDIX D

GAME ON – RELLAFIT SPARCS

(SPARC = Small Positive Act that Renews your Connection – to self, others, and life)

This Appendix contains six SPARCs that are part of the RellaFit (Relational Fitness) Challenge. The RellaFit Challenge is a game that is designed to turn what you have learned into real-life practices. This will help the knowledge move from your head to your heart and hands. If you want to play the full online version of the "A Walk with Lady Wisdom" RellaFit Challenge, go to www.rella.fit to learn more. To play this small sample of the game, read on.

Step 1: Get a Partner

To play the RellaFit Challenge, you need to find a partner. Nobody plays alone. Your partner must agree to either listen to the results of your SPARCs or complete all six SPARCs and share their results with you. Both people do not have to read the book.

Step 2: Complete the SPARCs

This sample version of the RellaFit Challenge contains six three-minute SPARCs. Follow the directions for each SPARC, complete it, and then write five to ten sentences that describe your experience. Your partner should do the same.

Step 3: Share Your Stories

Meet with your partner (either in person or on the phone) and share what you experienced while completing your SPARCs. If you are in person, each player signs their initials indicating that they did, in fact, complete the SPARC, and your partner signs their initials indicating that the results were discussed. Once both players have signed, the player receives five points for each completed SPARC (total of thirty points for all six SPARCs). To add some extra fun, create an incentive (financial, symbolic, etc.) to give to each player when all thirty points are earned.

SPARC LW-1A

Category: DignitySeeking

Name: Infinite Curiosity

Think of a person you know who you don't connect with very easily. What is a question you could ask that might help you connect with them better? Do they know something or have they done something that you haven't? (Hint: the answer is yes.) What is that, and how could you learn about it?

Contact them (in person, on the phone, or over email) and ask them one question to learn about some part of them that helps you see their deeper self. Write five to ten sentences describing what you learned.

Example: (Mary, 17, Ohio) *I decided to connect with my grandma because she isn't good with technology and likes to be face-to-face, but she isn't interested in anything that I am. The one thing I could think of was that I am trying to figure out my future, and so I asked her how she figured out what she wanted to do when she was my age. It was so great because I wrote her a short paper note with that question and she wrote me this long one…*

_____

_____

_____

_____

_____

_____

Player Initials: _____Partner Initials: _____5 points: _____

SPARC LW-2A

Category: Awakenings

Name: Being Salt

Think of a person who might benefit from learning something that you know that they don't. How could you help them become thirsty for a new good thing? Don't be the expert. What do you have that is not advice but provokes thirst for the good—a question, a story, an invitation? Don't give the answers. Let the thirst build and let them find the water. Try sharing your salt with someone and see how it goes.

Example: (Juan, 43, Colorado) *My relationship with my son hasn't been good since he turned 15. He almost seems to hate the sound of my voice. Advice goes nowhere, so I chose this SPARC. I decided to put an object in his room without any explanation. I chose this medal that my dad won in college. It was great. He was curious about who put it there and what it was all about...*

_____

_____

_____

_____

_____

_____

Player Initials: _____ Partner Initials: _____ 5 points: _____

SPARC LW-3A

Category: Human Insights

Name: Finding the Currency

Think of someone you know who is going through a hard time. Think of some questions you might ask them that would help you understand what they are going through. Create a gift for them that honors both where they are at and how you can help them move through it.

Example: (Katie, 18, Texas) *My dad has been a bit stressed lately. I gave him a certificate to give him a shoulder rub for 15 minutes. He redeemed it, and when I rubbed his shoulders I think it really made his day. He told me that...*

_____

_____

_____

_____

_____

_____

Player Initials: _____Partner Initials: _____5 points: _____

SPARC LW-4A

Category: Inner Core

Name: Having Gravity

What is it that helps you stay grounded? What beliefs, experiences, values, and characteristics do you have that, simply by being who you are, gives good to others? Create a list of three of these gifted parts of yourself. If you get stuck, ask someone who cares about you to help (you may want to do that anyway). Find some images online, from a magazine, or that you created that represent these important parts of yourself, and hang it in a place you look at regularly.

Example: (Carter, 22, New York) *I am at a place in life where I'm questioning the meaning of things: my job, my relationships, friends... This one helped me because I'm also visual. Having something to look at every day to remind myself what is important helped me say no...*

_____

_____

_____

_____

_____

_____

Player Initials: _____Partner Initials: _____5 points: _____

SPARC LW-5A

Category: Suffering Re-seen

Name: Off Tracks Strong

What's a good quality about yourself or a person you know that might have been twisted or misunderstood, and led them to a bad direction or pattern? You may want to use "Three Steps Out" to find the good behind seemingly negative emotions about the suffering. Often this good is connected to hidden or confused strengths.

Example: (Kathy, 53, California) *I have a lot of negative thoughts in my head about emotions because of how I was raised. I always feel like I'm too much to handle, so I end up pretending and doing what I think people want. The Three Steps Out exercise helped me see that it's because I like to see people happy and benefiting from me in their life that I do this kind of thing, and it's actually a good quality at heart...*

_____

_____

_____

_____

_____

_____

Player Initials: _____ Partner Initials: _____ 5 points: _____

SPARC LW-6A

Category: Wisdom Way Out

Name: Home Plant, Healthy Dirt

Choose someone who seems very different from you and ask them one question about their world and what might help you understand them better. Write your experience below.

Example: (Joel, 18, Kansas) *There is a guy at my work that drives me nuts. I just don't get him. So today I did this SPARC so I could figure out what makes him tick. He is Hispanic like me, so I decided to ask him about his family. This normally tough guy talked to me like I was an old friend! He loves his family, and work is just something to pay the bills...*

_____

_____

_____

_____

_____

_____

Player Initials: _____Partner Initials: _____5 points: _____

APPENDIX E

Guide to Healing Relationships

I am stepping out on a limb here. In calling for roles in the space between professional help and friendship, I risk being misunderstood and appearing to endorse what I do not. I came close to editing the "healing relationships" theme out of the book, but too many people have shown me that healing communities with culminating wisdom will not grow without them. Please recall the beginning of this book, where I state that this road is not for everyone and every place. If you are choosing to develop the capacities to navigate uncommon healing relationships despite the risks involved, this appendix is a start toward setting *some* limits and practices to avoid *some* pitfalls. It is setting some guideposts, not providing a guide. I am a part of some lovely experiments embracing this subject and see clearly that we all have a lot to learn in this domain.

Why health beyond the health system?

When relational poverty and mental health deprivation are endemic, we do not have the luxury to believe in the exclusive profession-alization of health. The implementation of the idea that health can primarily reside in an industry has never been a reality, and it is only recent delusions in human history that allow the potency of familial and communal nurture to have lost its place as health's prime locus.

The recovery of health-wisdom's roots in living systems cannot be limited to the professional realm. We are in greater need of healthful neighborhoods and wise local elders than we are of more psychiatrists. Perhaps reducing the need for medication and bolstering medication's benefits by cultivating communities rich in health skills would give us the long view on the matter. In order to blend our healing capacities in the personal and professional arenas, we must imagine new roles. We need the ability to acknowledge and support healthful practices that are already woven into communities. We need ways to encourage the passing of these gifts between generations. If we see isolation as the number one multiplier and amplifier of mental illness, we can begin to take such actions confidently.

We must now be intentional about our whole human formation so as to avoid being caught up in powerful forces (e.g. political fears and divisions, media addiction, etc.) which enticingly enact the inner impoverishment (the loss of depth) of broad swaths of generations. Intentional ethical, social, and spiritual growth does not have to be top-down and often is best when alongside (recall Sarah's story, the conclusion of this book, and RellaFit in Appendix D).

We often lack contexts for integrating wisdom across specialties. We often lack the capacity to take exploratory risks outside of specialties and into what is truly best for clients' and professionals' growth. In order to make these attempts we need to build deeper partnerships between professional health providers and local nonprofits, social, and religious organizations which are capable of remembering and passing on what is learned.

SOME FORMS OF HEALING FRIENDSHIP

There is a theme in the stories of our six women. The gains in freedom and recovery they made required a combination of real relationship and therapeutic understanding. This is the specific form I will be
addressing below, but before I do so I want to acknowledge similar
forms that may be less intentional, but also contain informal therapeutic skill and respectful relationship.

Using the Project I See You (ISY) organization as an example,
we can learn about the application of this way of being in its many
forms. These women thought they were going to be primarily
"providers of help" but instead became a functioning community
being woven into the existing communities of the Dominican Re-
public (DR) and inner city Denver, some interesting relational roles
emerged or were acknowledged as healing and vital:

- *Familial roles*—standing in for what was not given
  in a family—both for Americans and Domincans; both
  for those who are on the street and know poverty and
  those who have homes and know affluence

- *Mentors, Tio and Tia, "Uncle," "Auntie"*—a common
  role in many cultures which brings more healthy adults
  into the lives of children and adolescents;

- *Colleague friend*— Sharing professional knowledge to
  the need of a particular context; developing trust to take
  professional risks and safely share vulnerabilities and needs
  for learning;

- *Elder*—Affirming as vital those who were existing bearers of experience and wisdom in all contexts;

- *Soul Friend*—Anam Cara—A deep, transformative friendship among some of the core members of the organization (see the book by John O'Donohue by that name);

- *Adoption*—Some ISY American families legally adopted Dominican children as an outgrowth of the love that came from being welcomed into the Dominican community.

QUOTES ILLUSTRATING THESE ROLES

"We had an existing hope to adopt as an early part of our family life. We thought we would adopt in the United States but when we moved to the DR, we fell in love with the culture and the people and realized we would have the relationships we made there for the rest of our lives. It opened us up to international adoption to know that our child would have a knowledge of where they are from and continue to come back. We learned that the DR is such a communal place that adoption doesn't happen unless a child is abandoned. We were told that the legal process of adoption is difficult compared to other countries. But we chose it and would choose it again. Our decision was an extension of our love and has changed all of us."

"The friendships that formed as our lives melded together became forever friendships."

"One Dominican woman became a natural leader among us all and now runs a community center that we built together."

"When we felt that we were a part of the Dominican communities and saw these abandoned children, it was as if they were already inside us. To adopt a few into our families was a natural part of our desires that were shaped by being included and adopted by our Dominican friends."

How can we deny the deep healing power reflected in such statements that stand on hundreds of small choices and changes? Though we have so much abuse of intimacy in our time, we should not run from our universal need to give and receive it.

Professional roles can support such movements but cannot hold them in their entirety.

FINDING A ROLE THAT FITS

If we reflect on Sarah's discovery of using the role of barista to unexpectedly become a kind of counselor, we have some lessons on finding a role that fits the person and circumstances.

Prior to finding a role that fit, she reported that the expectations, rules, and forms of care-providing were crushing to her capacities of awareness. She had the positive template of the relationship with me that worked for her in high school, but had trouble replicating it in other places. She now describes her new role and context in the following ways:

- There is less weight of knowledge—I can keep a little distance to protect myself;

- I'm primarily a barista, but being a "mini-therapist" is a bonus;

- I love naturally knowing people in a place where they can relax;

- It's freeing to have covert knowledge and have total choice as to when to use it;

- There are many opportunities to connect if we both want, or to not connect if we prefer;

- No pressure!

- If I'm upset because I feel something from a person, I can disengage without guilt;

I also noticed:

- She doesn't have to show progress to justify how her time is spent regarding healing others;

- She doesn't have to perform;

- There is no one to disappoint, nor expectations to fail to meet;

- There is honesty in relating;

- She does not feel like an object to be used by others.

It took multiple "failures" to find what did not fit her needs, but changing the role and conditions have allowed Sarah to thrive and provide more to the people around her.

GUIDING HEALING FRIENDSHIP PRACTICES

There are risks in melding professional health roles with the natural power of authentic relationship. Here are some lessons I have learned through many attempts:

- This is not a practice for the inexperienced or the very stressed;

- This does not fit most institutions as they currently operate;

- All roles can be abused. All trust bonds are as risky as the intimacy is strong and as the needs and wounds are able to rise up to overpower good limits. This does not mean that we should avoid bonds of trust—the more true ones that are available, the fewer false ones will have the power to appear trustworthy and do harm.

- There are legitimate places for protected relationships. What the medical model preserves is important for a larger system. Boundaries are important—dual relationships and transference are legitimately risky and can be harmful.

- Sometimes friendship is necessary for healing. Friendship has many forms and degrees, as illustrated above, and it is necessary to recognize that all levels can be respectful and offer dignity.

• I befriend *some* clients only under *some* circumstances—but to all I offer true relationship. Even with the most mentally ill and dangerous people I have met with, I can find grounding, real material to offer and receive, which is a part of me and a part of them. When the risks are higher, I might share little direct information about my life beyond a peaceful, connecting, listening presence. Often fewer words are a great gift to someone who is living in high stress or inner chaos.

• As a time- and energy-limited being, I must choose who I will share my limited self with and who I will receive from.

• I have chosen not to work under the medical model for many reasons. One is that because some exceptional client relationships are powerful and important. In the abundance they create, many are served beyond the initial healing relationship. Suffering is transformed from a victim position to a wisdom position when what has been experienced is used beneficially, and lagging skills that may be linked to the suffering are honestly addressed.

• Suffering itself is not an automatic gateway to wisdom, and elevating people too quickly to service roles based on their suffering can cause harm. Sarah needed understanding, practice, support, and a good fit to transform her combination of strengths and struggles into a method that worked for her. Similar elements are needed for most of the people I have known who make the transition from suffering to wisdom.

A friend who is a small-town pastor with a big heart illustrates some ways to keep safe when intimacy is unavoidable. You cannot hide as easily when your group is smaller and your role is, by its nature, a close part of the lives of the people you work with. When he meets with a potentially risky person he reminds himself, "This is a real relationship—all relationships have limits and risks." He uses his role to set the stage for both connection and limitation. A small-town pastor plays many roles and relates on many levels. At times he will actually say, "I am putting on my pastor hat" or "I am asking your professional opinion" to show what roles are being utilized. As a compassionate person, it was initially challenging for him to embrace the following advice from someone who had been a pastor longer: "It's a job. Don't sacrifice family; don't go too far." Seeing his role as a job despite the many real relationships involved eventually helped him set a framework that was protective and genuinely connecting. It allowed room to stop thinking about people in his "work" when he needed rest.

Helping professions are always a blend of self and other. Finding ways to open and close wisely in these relationships is vital to long term well-being.

SAFEGUARDS

Examples of Grounding Beliefs:

- My family and work are more important than any amount of short-term pleasures.

- No safeguard is foolproof, and no rule without loopholes.

- The level of risk must be known clearly and, if high, shared and borne with others.

- Every relationship has boundaries; determining what works for each one is important.

- Good people fall down far in the midst of these grey areas of intimacy.

- Meeting emotional needs is powerful and the limits must be equally powerful.

Develop Capacities for Higher Local Accountability

It is much easier to trick a system or a representative of a system if they have some distance from the reality they are monitoring. Welcoming perceptive people into the risky details of uncommon relating is vital to keeping it healthy. Here are examples of practices which can help:

- Having a person or people who are able to check any communication or messaging system that you utilize within the limits of pre-established confidentiality agreements;

- Establishing trusted colleague consultations (rather than just required ones) as a regular habit for tricky situations;

- Investing time in honest, close relationships with the power to see and sense when they are unhealthy. These are vital to avoiding foolishness that might otherwise be accidentally embraced. There are always things we can't see in relationships.

- Attraction—Be honest, and run your thinking past someone who knows you well enough to see if you are tricking yourself. Sometimes less blatant attraction is more risky because it's more easily missed.

- Asking discerning questions regularly, such as

- Is a need being met in this relationships that is harming/detracting from my core relationships?

- Developing power-intimacy awareness;

  – Power and intimacy are often connected;
  – Both receiving affirmations of power and relinquishing ower can be intimate;
  – Physical touch of any kind is intimate and expresses power (not automatically bad, but must add to awareness);
  – Age and perceived status differences (the movie *Mr. Holland's Opus* contains some good examples of how this can be attractive and hollow).

CHALLENGES IN ROLE AND LIMIT SETTING

It is tempting to create a list of rules to keep relationships on a good track. I have included here some examples from the lives around me (presented in the first-person form) which illustrate why this is not easy.

- "Sometimes things that establish role are helpful like age difference, growing a beard, or wearing role-related clothes to show the operating space." At times this can actually do the opposite, as appearance related to uniforms or authority can be attractive.

- "My marriage being strong helps to reduce my desire to meet my needs elsewhere." However, security and stability can lead to a desire to try new things and take risks.

- "Sometimes a well-placed window in the door can largely preserve confidentiality but provide the ability for someone to look in if needed." On other occasions, any such window will prevent a person from feeling comfortable or can give a false sense of security when what is being said is more dangerous than what is being done.

There are many resources for further development of safeguards (topical suggestions: professional ethics, boundaries, interdependency, etc.), but the point here is to see the limits to an autonomous, individual approach.

FORMAL COUNSELING

In allowing for some of these alternative forms and knowing how to empower and nurture them, we can return to professional counseling and psychological supports. Knowing what each option can and cannot do helps to understand what they uniquely offer and which may be needed.

- In counseling there can be a place where there aren't confusing attachments if healthy attachments have not been experienced.

- There may need to be a place outside of everyday life

to learn to see differently, understand life history differently, or to practice relational skills which are hard to enact inside current patterns.

• There are many examples where the professional/client relationship must be formal and protected for things such as safety, high relational or attachment confusion, or overwhelming stressors. This does not mean humanity or real relating cannot be selectively included, but to do so may require great care and intentionality.

• Diagnoses, medication, and homeopathy do not teach skills, but they can help a person gain some peace, some improved mood, or increased focus to be able to do the work necessary for long-term growth.

To Know We Are On the Right Path

Here are some quotes from people who have given and received healing friendship to illustrate the potential good if done well:

"I needed the refreshing 'of course' that you often gave as I told my life story. It showed me why I had made the choices I made and why I had to break the box of my old beliefs. You showed me that I made sense."

"Where do you get your people? I want friends like those that you have that back you up and strengthen you."

"When you reflect back to me what you see in the tangle of words that I give you, it simplifies my dilemmas."

"You gave me a new perception of how things can be done
Let's be at peace with each other
Let's talk as if we are friends and close
Gave each other perceptions
Someone to walk with."

"In order to enter into deeper relationship one's wounds must be fully accepted as they are and demonstrated to not be a threat to the relationship. For the relationship to grow deeper still, the wounds must be separated from the identity. This can lead to the confusion that the person is now unaccepted - that the wound is not legitimate – and that the protection strategies are foolish. It might bring up fear that the relationship never was good or valid. It takes patient endurance to allow the separation to happen and be okay."

"Real transformative relating can be risky
Being unlocked and awakened is powerful
It can cause the one who is involved with the freeing
to be given too much adoration
Who has done the most work
It is the wounded one
The guide gives light touches which shift and shape
But it is [the] wounded one who truly labors, suffers,
       endures, risks, steps into the unknown, faces fears, faces

rejection, finds lost treasures and new treasures
The guide reflects with (as it can only be), discovers with,
    celebrates with,
Offers insight into what already is and what can be
Offers experiences outside of the wounded's scope
But it the wounded who embrace, accepts, softens, changes,
The courage lies there
The guide should be seen as a collector of stories and sights
Which are liberating treasures to be shared
But they are often not their own
And should be known as such."

"We are all wounded by life
We all need replenishment
It is in the deepest of our relationships
That our recovery is found
Re-finding, refilling, reworking –
All needed to reach refining
Working smarter requires
Being different
Only those with access to our soft center
Can equip enduring change."

It is my hope that the vital power of healing relationships is honored. Reciprocal dignity can be a gateway to wisdom and wisdom can open the way to deeper reciprocal dignity. To create these rich, abundant cycles, we cannot be blind to the hazards that can cause good relationships to become harmful. Let us learn, ask for help, and open ourselves to hearing truth in love that can prepare us to be ready recipients of these gifts.

About the Author

Eric has worked in social enterprise, theatre, organizational consulting, education, and a range of health capacities. These experiences have brought him into close relationship with people in many walks of life. Is it any surprise that his writings honor those on the edges of life - those who cross the dividing lines in order to find meaningful ways to bring light into dark places?